A *College Journal* of

John Gardner

Introduction by

Thomas Gavin

The University of Rochester Libraries 1999

Library of Congress No. 98-61693
ISBN: 0-9665639-0-5 Limited Edition
ISBN: 0-9665639-1-3 Cloth
ISBN: 0-9665639-2-1 Paperback

Second Printing

University of Rochester Libraries
University of Rochester
Rochester, New York, 14627-0055

CONTENTS

THE TEACHER TEACHING HIMSELF

In September of 1952, a nineteen-year-old sophomore at DePauw University, with his fiancee Joan reading over his shoulder, browses through Katherine Mansfield's journal and realizes how to get more out of his own journal. His very first gesture is significant: he announces that he has "a doozy cold" and describes his runny nose in five distinct voices—terse, bombastic, despairing, resigned, and existential ("The red nose simply exists"). In the following days, as he records the prankish doings of friends in his dorm hall, the journal is vivid, to be sure, but as callow as any undergraduate journal has a right to be. The October 10 entry, however, is a long attack on the failure of verisimilitude in Defoe's *Moll Flanders,* and from this point on the journal—published now in a facsimile edition by the University of Rochester Libraries—holds to a steady purpose: it is the workshop in which John Gardner teaches himself the craft that will make him one of the great writer-teachers of his time.

With the journal shaping his discipline, Gardner as teacher is his own best student. He writes character sketches, scenes, poems, parodies, polemics arguing with critics and teachers—then tests and questions his own words (he calls the journal *Lies! Lies! Lies!* to remind himself that his opinions are provisional). Again and again he formulates strategies that he will incarnate in novels and pass on to other writers in lectures and books on the writer's craft. The journal's several descriptions of a runny nose, for example, will come as no surprise to anyone in the audience for the first of his many fiction lectures at the Bread Loaf Writers' Conference.

"A good writer," he said then, "knows half a dozen ways to write any scene. He's practiced them all the way a musician practices scales, till he's mastered the whole range of his instrument."

This passion for the craft, which Gardner on another occasion called "the only religion I know," was part of what made him an electrifying teacher.

By the time of that 1974 Bread Loaf lecture, he wore his authority at a rakish tilt that made his teaching a performance as well as a feast of insights. Three days into the conference Gardner hadn't yet been seen. The writers creaking the folding chairs in the Little Theater had been waiting nearly twenty minutes; rumors breezed around the room that he'd had car trouble and wouldn't be coming. Then in the parking lot tires crunched the gravel, the theater screen-door swung wide, and before it clapped shut a stocky man in a black leather vest and full-sleeved peasant shirt strode to the podium. His shoulder-length hair was shock-white, as if he'd been groomed by a lightning bolt. He cast over the audience the blue-eyed glare his monster Grendel might aim at a meadhall filled with hostile Danes, and said, "I'm a medievalist, I don't know anything about this crap." Then he grinned, as comfortable now as we were puzzled, and for the next hour contradicted himself, tossing out double handfuls of insights into the craft of fiction like a dragon giving away his gold.

Though none of us that day could have known how his youthful journal helped to forge the disciplines he was outlining, we had no trouble believing that the demands he casually laid on us were demands he made on himself.

"You need to read <u>everything</u>," he said. "And writers don't read only for pleasure. They <u>ravage</u> what they read—rip the guts open and figure out how the masters worked their tricks."

Which is exactly what, in his sophomore journal, we see him doing.

He is stimulated as much by what he mistrusts as by what he admires. Reading *Moll Flanders,* Gardner scorns Defoe for being so besotted with his heroine that when he describes Moll's meeting with the first love of her youth he forgets that by this point in her history she is a woman of sixty-five, raddled by a life of petty theft, prostitution, and stretches in Newgate prison.

"Just for fun," Gardner muses, "I think I'll burlesque the passage I quoted . . . ." Speaking as Moll, he writes:

> "My dear," croaks I, "do you not know me?" He turned pale, and
>
> started retching, like one thunderstruck in the belly, and not able to

conquer his odorous vomiting, said no more but this, "Let us sit

down!" and sitting down by a table he laid his elbow upon his plate

of beans and potatoes, and hanging his chin off his hand, fixed his

eyes on his nose as one stupid. I cried so vehemently, on the other

hand, that it was a good while ere I could speak anymore; but after I

had given some vent to my amourous passion (for 65 is not as old as

you think) I stopped crying and let him go, saying "My dear, do you

not know me?" At which he puked some more and answered,

"Glurgle," and said no more for a good while.

The first point to note here is that before burlesquing the passage Gardner has *copied* it longhand into his journal. Though at the moment Gardner isn't appreciating the driving energy that makes Defoe's sentences hypnotic; by *copying* them—and then *studying* them well enough to parody them—he absorbs their rhythms, makes their possibilities permanently his own. It's this kind of alchemy Gardner will speak of in *The Art of Fiction* when he advises the young writer to get "the art of fiction, in all its complexity—the whole tradition and all its technical options—down through the wrinkles and tricky wiring of his brain into his blood." It's also worth mentioning that in the margin of this entry we see Gardner criticizing his own excesses. With an arrow pointing toward the line in which Moll's first lover pukes and then glurgles, he writes: "Like when Pope lets his disgust drown out his wit."

The journal, then, gives its writer a chance to discover what works and what doesn't. The motto on its first page is: "if it's worth telling / it's worth stretching." But on page 11, after a five-page rendering of undergraduates short-sheeting beds, taking the screws out of doorknobs and plastering them with toothpaste, he writes, "I see that I was wrong in thinking that a good story is better when stretched." Boring himself with expansion, Gardner learns the virtue of brevity.

Gardner was convinced that writers learn by reading—a practice too often neglected by novices whose sense of language and human potential comes to them packaged by television hucksters. He speaks (again in *The Art of Fiction*) of Melville working to wring meaning from his narrative of a whaling voyage: ". . . he happens to read Shakespeare and some philosophy books at the same time, and because of his reading he hits on heretofore unheard-of solutions to problems of novelistic exploration."

To understand how Gardner hit on a few of his own solutions, we need only read of his youthful admiration for Fielding's *Tom Jones.* In the journal:

> "[Critic William Lyon] Phelps says [Fielding] slowed down the progress of the novel by advocating digressions at the beginning of each book in a work. Me, I wish novelists would do it some more. Those digressions don't in the least tempt me to skip. They build suspense, and at the same time please me with their thoughtfulness. His books become one long (886 pages for Tom Jones) essay. Never at any time does the author leave the stage. He becomes a sage with a $3 seat making clever comments as the play progresses. Reading Fielding is like going to a good play with someone who knows it well. Between the acts we have delicious commentary on the thing. It's great! I swear, if I can ever become a writer (and I can, because I like this sort of thing) I shall—when my fame is established—take up the style of Fielding."

With this passage in mind we can imagine Gardner, more than a decade later, pulling his well-underlined college edition of *Tom Jones* off the shelf as he broods over a novel on the Beowulf theme; he spends a few minutes refreshing his pleasure in the book's mock-epic structure, and decides he can use the same epic division of parts in Grendel. A couple of years later he reaches again for his Fielding, and realizes that he just might get away with regularly suspending the flow of a novel's action while two characters engage in Socratic dialogues on a wide range of cultural and philosophical issues—and suddenly the structure of *The Sunlight Dialogues* snaps into place.

Seldom has an undergraduate made such fruitful use of the books on his required-reading list. He admires *Humphrey Clinker* and *The Vicar of Wakefield*, quarrels violently with Thackeray, whom he hates "with a beautiful blood-dripping hate" because he spoke slightingly of Gardner's great love, Jonathan Swift. Gardner admires *Gulilver's Travels* so much that he devotes a long entry to outlining its structure. Another begins with the observation that "when we are happy . . . we float on our joy and any serious thought is beneath us. The men who make great advances . . . are the suffering Carlyle; the rheumatic Matthiew Brambles: the oppressed Dostiefskis; the hypochondriactic Johnsons." From that premise, he outlines a series of proposals—in the spirit of Swift's bitterly ironic "Modest Proposal"—for making mankind miserable in order to create "the most supremely intellectual society in the history of the world." With Swift as his touchstone, he announces his ambition: "I know that if I were given one year, I could write a book on satire in the English novel, 1704–1900 . . . a book that must be written someday, for all critical studies of the English novel must be based on a good knowledge of my subject. The whole evolution of the novel rests on the genius of satire . . . . I have it all organized. But I must read and read and read."

What gets in the way of his reading, of course, is his education. He has to hurry his outline of *Gulliver* in order to study French. He has to spend five hours a week in a chemistry lab where he's criticized for his "sloppy lab procedure." Ultimately his impatience with the formal requirements that get in the way of his true learning erupts: "I don't want your slimy degree. I want stuff I can use when I want to write."

The journal trails off toward the end of the fall semester, but by then it has effected in its author a profound metamorphosis. He has learned that putting words on paper, even describing an ephemeral mood, creates a second self. "This mood," he writes, "has stepped out of me, become more real than myself. He sits over there in my chair reading Clarissa and chain smoking my cigarettes . . . Now and then he glances up at me with a smile that may be meant to mock. 'Whatter you laughing at?' I say, and he grins wide and says, 'something I read,' and he looks at me cornerwise so I know he's lying." This sly Double is the writer's most trustworthy friend, the one who peers over his shoulder at his every word with the critic's canny detachment. By December 9 the youth who began with the motto, "if it's worth telling, it's worth stretching," has taught himself so thoroughly that he can squint sidelong at one of his own paragraphs, and observe, "This is such a small thought it isn't worth condensing."

The journal's last pages show him experimenting with poetry: fragments of poems called "Mermaid," "On Thinking" (in ottava rima), "Atlantis." Finally, a page headed "The Human Hand" that contains no words, only stress marks for a poem in amphibrachic tetrameter. Even without any words fleshing this phantom hand, I recognized the hand that marked the scansion. I'd seen it before.

In 1974, midway in a draft of my novel, *Kingkill,* I went for the second year in a row to the Bread Loaf Writers' Conference, where John Gardner was my staff critic. He read a hundred-page chunk from the middle of the book and assured me it would find a publisher. Then—what was most generous for a teacher besieged with student manuscripts—he asked to see the beginning of the novel. Next day he handed it back. "The story's fine," he said, "but somewhere between last year and this you taught your- self a hell of a lot about rhythm. When you revise this first section, you'll have to fix the rhythms."

"Rhythm?" I said. "I thought only poets worried about rhythm."

"Think some more," he said.

Later I sat down with the first section beside the more recent pages; I saw that he'd marked stresses over some of the lines. Before long I realized that where the line was rhythmically slack, it was also dull—heavy with polysyllables and abstractions, words that filled out the syntax without shaping an image. In the early draft I often used up the thought of a sentence in a main clause that dragged subordinate clauses after it the way Marley's ghost drags his chains and cashboxes. Somehow in the months since I'd written those chapters, I'd learned that a thought should *hover* through a sentence, then stoop like a hawk at the end.

When I asked myself how I'd learned without knowing it, the answer came quickly. Every day, before I settled to write, I would read a few pages of *Wise Blood* or one of Flannery O'Connor's stories, just to get in my ear the sound of her whip-crack sentences. By the following summer, I'd worn out and replaced two copies of my paperback *Three by Flannery O'Connor*.

Gardner told me what I'd learned. Making me *aware* of what I'd absorbed from O'Connor "through the wrinkles and tricky wiring of [my] brain" gave me the power to use it consistently. It was a great gift, one that he could give me because he'd learned it himself, with a journal called *Lies! Lies! Lies!* as his teacher.

—Thomas Gavin
Rochester, New York

A NOTE ON THE TEXT

John Gardner's college journal, *Lies! Lies! Lies!* is presented here in a facsimile edition in the author's hand. Although the author's penmanship is generally clear, the facsimile pages are followed by a typeset version of the same text. In the interest of remaining faithful to the original, spellings and grammatical errors were not corrected in the typset pages, and are presented here essentially without editing.

The facsimile images were reduced from the original manuscript by approximately 15% to accommodate the format of this edition.

This journal was essentially a college student's notebook, and the main body of the text was followed in the original by exercises in verse writing. While these exercises will be of interest to the reader, and are reproduced here, it was the decision of the publisher neither to transcribe them nor to reproduce blank pages that fell between. There are, therefore, gaps in the original folio numbers in those pages.

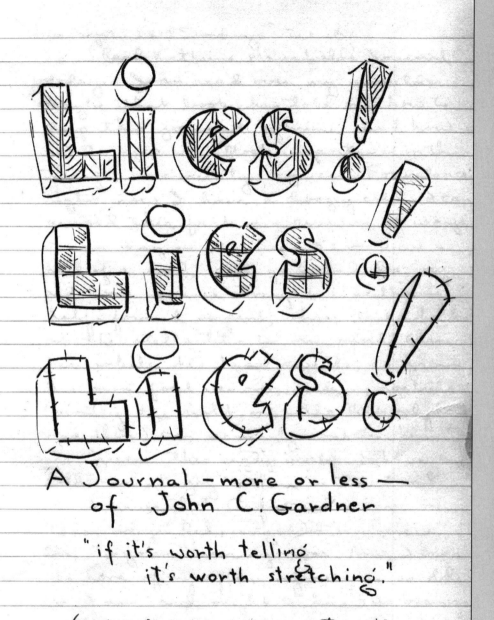

Lies! Lies! Lies!

A Journal — more or less —
of John C. Gardner

"if it's worth telling
it's worth stretching."

(or in language of a senator; "Lies,
villifications, filthy, ~~dry~~ slimy gossip!)

education vs. learning

'26 Sept. '52 ; Sunday

Read Kathrine Mansfield's Journal
today. Joan read over my shoulder.
Maybe that book has told me how to
keep this journal of mine. And how
not to keep it. / Most important in this
thing, is sincerity, I guess. For instance,
right now I have a doozey cold. I can
record this fact in a number of ways.
I can say — "26 Sept. '52 — Have a
hell of a cold," and go to bed. Or, "my
red nose houses tonight a slithering,
half-formed serpent, whose tail whacks
at the stellactites in my mind's chamber, while his head swells, as from
his own foul venom, till my nostrils
(mostly the right one — the left only now
and then) can scarcely contain him."
Or, "Curse this ugly world. I have a
cold. What joy is there in life? and
what reward? A fie and a pox on
this unguided, ungodded universe."
Or, "I got a runny nose. Now, I know
it's none of my affair; my nose is as old
as I am and ought to know its business
by this time; but it sure makes kissing
awkward. Next time, friend nose, please choose
to run when we're in Greencastle

instead of here in St Louis. Better still, take a tip from this year's presidential candidates and don't run at all till I ask you. (And don't get your hopes up, cause I won't — unless there's a Rotary test I wanta miss.)"

Now if I sincerely feel any one of these, I'll write it. But at the moment I'd write nothing at all. I have no sentiments concerning the matter. The red nose simply exists.

I said before that I must be sincere. I didn't quite mean all that that might imply. After all, my joy is my dishonesty. I will be true to my mood — and I _am_ a moody child. But as to facts . . . .

When I was younger I used to worry about my fibs. I thought I would surely burn for them one day. But now that I am older and have read Robert Browning and Mickey Spillane, I am not afraid. I consider lies life, and vice versa. How horribly dull would be a day on a tractor with no human within a mile, if one could not stretch the basic truth of his life to wild, yet believable, stories.

I used to frighten Bill — my mental and physical elder, with tales of how "Johnny Mills and me saw the ghost" — up in the overgrown, forgotten cemetery behind Kenny Lowell's.

I will say, it's unfortunate that nobody can believe me anymore. Even Jack, the closest friend I've got (who else, of any sex, would meet me at 4 a.m. at a station one mile — on foot yet — out of town*. And me coming home from a most routine two day trip. Greater love hath no man.) As I was saying, even Jack always gives me a chance to say I was joking when I tell him some silly, reasonless fib. But of course I always swear on my honor that they're true. Sometimes I swear to things that really are true. Life is very complex.

   Still, I can be true to character in writing. I won't misrepresent anybody. But as to what they do — so, they can't remember it.

← MY MUSE   (Come thou ... muse)

* Roger Getty came too. Of this lad this book will hear more!

29 - Sept. 52 - Monday

    I must not leave my little roommate alone on weekends. It is not safe.

    This weekend when I returned from St. Louis I found Locust Manor in a gentle uproar.

    Right off the bat let it be understood that my boy Gooseberry (muh-roommate) never does anything naughty unless somebody else gives him the idea. Little Jackie _could_ be very innocent.

    Harold A. Petersen is a house councellor in Locust Manor. Roger Getty is a sweet fella who never did anything more malicious than blow up a dietition's automobile ('in 1951).

    Said Harold A. Petersen to Roger Getty in the hearing of John Robert (Goose-)Berry, "This place is too quiet."

    Said Roger Getty, "Uh-huh."

    Said Pete, "Somebody should short-sheet some beds, or take screws out of doorknobs, or something."

    In the half hour that superceeded this delightful conversation, that is, while counsellor Petersen, studied industriously, Mr Getty and The Goose occupied themselves with short-sheeting beds in the attic where we sleep, piling unused mattresses on the bed of one Wheel Barrow, polishing door handles with gobs of toothpaste (Colgate), owned by the Goose, and taking screws out of numerous door-knobs, including that which is attatched to the public phone on the second floor of this noble building. For the information of this journal, a door-knob with the screw taken out will turn round and round in the hand of him who wants in, or out, making no impression upon the latch of the door.

↑
le goose

Upon completing the numerous businesses mentioned above, Misters Getty and Berry went downstairs to push buzzers (which call the occupants of this our dormatory to the phone). One by one, the boys came out, their hands dripping toothpaste, their angry mouths dripping foam. and profanity. Not to be left out, Misters Getty and Berry swore and dripped with the rest.

At bed time, (close to midnight in this place) while Mr. Petersen slept, in came —

Mr. Z——, who had just had a battle with the love of his life. Ready for tears, this lad. And, upon jumping into his sabotaged bed, ready to express more tangible emotion.

Mr. A——, whose mottoe seems to be,

'speak loudly while battling 'em down with yer big stick. (He battled down, among other innocents, Mr Z___, who lay softly cursing universal powers — like Mr Clapp who should be on the job times like these.)

When Barrow, who doesn't mind sleeping on six mattresses unless his pillow happens to be at the bottom of them. (A real princess, this.)

Mr F___, who saw the humor of it all. (He'd make a good frat man. He's cute.)

Mr W___, who immediately considered this a matter for the house council. (Not till morning tho'.)

And so on, into the night.

At six a.m., when the last straggler came in (myself — just off the train), Mr W___, a light sleeper, had had enough.

"Pete," screeched he, shaking the sleeping bones of our councellor, "It's time we took some action!"

And so, at six-thirty, a very solemn house meeting was had by all. Unfortunately there are no minutes of this meeting, since our secretary is a heavy sleeper, even while sitting up in bed with a notebook in his hand.

"Fellow residents," droned Mr. Petersen, looking

unhappily (and fruitlessly) for his pillow, "It has been brought to my attention that somebody has pulled a nasty. Now I happen to know the names of the instigators of this nonsense, and if that person, or those persons, will step forward at this time, no great harm will be done them."

(Pete didn't rise himself, so Getty and the Goose sat in their places.)

"Very well, then we shall consider the matter closed." Upon which words Mr. Petersen lay back without his pillow.

Mr. W——— had other ideas which he voiced without timidity.

"Oh all right," grumbled Pete after a brutal shaking, "If you think it that important I'll go to Kent and tell all." Very patiently, then, our councellor went over + over the probable punishment and resultant unhappiness of all persons in the dorm until Mr. W——— said he was heartily sorry for his hasty indignation, and forgave the "harmless pranksters."

When the meeting broke up Mr. Berry found it necessary to telephone a friend to explain why he had missed his appointment with her at Marion Springs.

At ten-thirty when I went by the
telephone booth he was still there,
looking very sad and bluish, making signs
at the door-knob. I waved at him as I passed.

When I came in from classes at 3 pm I
found the Goose still in the booth. (I don't
know what went on between times, so I can't
tell you.) On the window there was a sign
reading:

To whoever It may Concern:

Under normal conditions this
is a public telephone booth, but
due to the acute housing shortage
the assholes of this university decided
this should be a private room.

In there with him I saw (though much
smoke) a box of candy (mine), a pack of
cigarettes, a notebook and some envelopes,

Outside the door sat Mr. Getty, blowing the smoke of chlorophyll cigarettes through the key-hole. Says Pete with great authority, "Quiet hours!" whenever M. Berg's screaming becomes audible through the panel. Says Mr. E. passing by, "That looks like a nice place. He should live about two days, anyway." And says Mr. Getty, "If there develops a shortage of air in there, don't breath so much."

That's all I know.

(To all this I solemnly swear.)

30 - Sept. 52 - Tuesday -

Who put lighter fluid in the toilet bowls? Next time I'm gonna put my cigarette in an ash tray.

1 - October - 52 - Wednesday -

I begin to think this journal a good idea. I admit, at first I thought it a bit silly; but now I've changed my opinion. It is becoming a log of Locust Manor. In it I can record all the gay, crazy, friendly pranks — the serious thoughts — the strange, unbelievable close moments we have here. And I see that I was wrong in thinking that a good story is better when stretched.

[But then, I had other reasons for saying the stories were elongated. For one thing, protection. Nobody can be held responsible for crimes I have recorded (with no malicious intent toward the criminals) as long as I say, "oh, that was just a story." So I won't say these things are true. No, maybe they're not!]

Perhaps I ought to apologize to the whiteness of this page for useing some of the words I'll use — and have already used. But there is good humor in some of them, I think. Besides, this is a men's dorm. I'll not dress it to look like Golin in April. No, by Gosh!

This is getting ridiculous.
On September the 28th the Goose and I put a typewritten sign on our door:
    GARDNER & BERRY ENTERPRISES.
That night a new sign decorated our port.
    GARDNER & BERRY ENTERPRISES
      PAY THE MADAM
On the 29th another new sign (on another

typewriter, elite type):

      GARDNER AND BERRY ENTERPRISES

         ARE <u>YOU</u> SAVED?

On the 30th:

      GARDNER AND BERRY ENTERPRISES

    We ask all consultants: are you WORTH saving?

Then tonight:

      GARDNER AND BERRY ENTERPRISES

Will the sonovabitch who changed this sign please

      do it again?

Somebody's naughty, I'd say.

Someone should re-spell the dictionary. Everybody
talks about it — Shaw for example, but we
still have to follow the old. Some of us more
closely than others.

The Monon script *The Serpent & the Dove* — went in
tonight. I like it. I just found out there's
fifty bucks for the winning team. Now I'll
worry. All I <u>really</u> hope is that Uncle Bobby's
five night masterpiece doesn't beat out my
twelve full months of concientious work.
(What are full months? Cliché? Besides, they're
<u>not</u> full. Some are 28 days, some 31, and
some have some other number, I understand.
I don't pay much attention. It seems to

me we oughtta start over. Yes, that's a good idea. What we need is a good war. I can say this, for I'm a phoole. Wiser men only approve war as a last resort. [spelling again. In the dictionery "resort" has to do with entertainment.] End parenthasies →.)

2-October-52 Thursday-

He's a good man. All wise, all sweet, all compassionate. His head bobs and his smile blooms like the head and smile of a bright-painted puppet in a wind tunnel. Or like a deaf-mute waiter trying to keep his job. He cocks his head and listens. Cocks it (click) like a batter waiting for a pitch. But in this case the baseball is not a baseball, but a gem out of the mouth of a suckling. (I'm he.) Don't you just love gems of wisdom? Well, you ponder this one. Me, I'm going to bed.

— COLD TEA —

I can't understand this hot tea business.

"Dave, excuse me, but I wonder if you could run up and get me some hot tea? This is cold."

"Sure, ma'am. Be right with you."

"Hot, now. Not warm. Hot!"

"Yes'm."

She smiles at me. Her eyes glance down her nose, followed by the lids. You'd call it coy on a younger woman.

"That's the one thing about this place," she says. "The tea is never hot. I just can't stand cold tea."

"Neither can I," I say. I'm a conformist. A polite conversationalist. Crude people would say "why can't you stand cold tea?" That's why they're crude, you know. They don't mind if the tea doesn't eat out their throats. But not I. I smile and say, "Neither can I."

Dave isn't there at all. A good waiter. His arm puts the cupful of steam in front of her.

"Oh thank you, David! Thank you!" She holds the seething stuff to her lips and sniffs it. "Oh that's good!" she says. Then she puts it down and waits for it to cool.

I sit and watch with half closed eyes and nearly casual eyebrows, like one of King Mythrandites' courtiers waiting for the soup to take its effect. I'm curious. But, as I say, not crude. My father told me all about sex, baseball, war, liquor — things like that. But he never said much about the peculiarities of nice society.

He was a simple farmer. He didn't even know the seven rules for picking up crumpets. Well, I am out to learn, so I must watch.

I watch.

"Have you decided what you'll be when you graduate, John?" No move to the cup.

"I'm not sure, ma'am." (smile) "With the world situation what it is...."

"Oh I know!" (sigh) Right hand dunks the tea-bag. In and out. In and out. A green ticket hooked to a white string - suddenly turning yellow about half way down. "No boy can plan anything these days."

"No ma'am."

"Will you be going to St. Louis again this week?"

"I think so. Jack too, if he gets his work done."

"That's nice." She's taking it now! In her hand! She drinks it - eyeing me cornerwise. I remember I'm staring. I look down. It doesn't matter. It's cold now.

And then I know that I am only a farmer, like my dad, and his dad, and his. One must be bred in society to understand it. Is it because a true blue-blood has a throat of Tungston steel and must show it to all? No. The tea got cold. Was it because, in olden times the master had to keep the servant busy?

"Is everyone finished?" She pushes back from the table. Bob, with a disinterested air, helps her rise. Cultured, that boy. But I don't know. I always used to kinda like some of the crude men and women who submitted, without thought, to cold tea. College is disillusioning, isn't it. All I can say is, I'm glad I'm young enough to learn new ways.

No thanks Clement. ~~You're~~ I can't take your cigarette. In the first place your not a frat man, and in the second, it hasn't got a filter. Third, what would I do with the lucky I'm smoking?

3 - October - 52 - Friday.

Some day I must write a satire on Reader's Digest condensations. A three page book (profusely illustrated with those Mother Goose type illustrations common to that magazine) for busy readers who don't care what the writer really wanted to say. I'll maybe call it ~~the~~ Can mutiny. Short sentences and fragments. Real ugly.

8 October – 1952 –

I was just serenely in bed when the door sneaked open. In crept two black shadows. I could not see, in the darkness, who lived in the black hulks, but I had no fear, for there are none but sweet, gentle souls in Locust Manor.

For a long time the shadows crouched at the foot of the bed next to mine – whispering and giggling. Then they became silent. I almost thought them worried. But I made no move, for I was dog-tired and needed my sleep. At length, one of the shadows moved forward and patted the bed next to me. Some hurried whispers followed. Then the shadows examined the bed where I slept. I saw the faces then. The Goose and another. They were pained faces. Wretched.

"Hey, Bud," whispered the Goose, nudging me. "Yer in my bed!"

"Oh! I must have counted wrong in the dark," I muttered, and rolled over.

My last recollection was of Jack sobbing by my bed (the right one, that is) while he and the other shook the sheets and re-made the bed. On the floor I heard the patter of tiny feet. Mice, I think; and the rattle of falling crumbs.

You don't understand, do you.

No wonder Kathrine Mansfield sobbed
on every page of her journal "I can't get
anything written." How can you write
other things if you spend all your time
on a journal?

(The philosopher)

When I have a child I shall give him white
shoes as soon as he learns to kick his feet.
Everybody who is somebody wears white shoes.
I can't afford a fraternity, but by goss I'm
getting my white bucks tomorrow.

9 October 52 - Thurs.   [For Joan's SLIM magazine]
    Here's a note to all yóse freshmens:
    Compliments make good impreshens.
    Shakespeare saith, when out to tea:
    "Lord, what foods these morsels be!"
                    — Noggin Gnash.

10 October -52 Friday.
    Moll Flanders surprised me. I thought it
would be fairly blah, but....
    Moll Flanders is 328 (Everyman's Edition) pages
of unparalleled, incomparable, unrivaled, unbelievable
uninhibited rot. A stronger, more disgusting word
would fit here, but no thanx. Blame the silly

representation of character upon the times, and take what's left. Blame the wandering, bouncing, impossible plot on Defoe's own full life, and take what's left. Blame the soaked handkerchiefs and red eyes on the "demand of the market for sentimentalism," and take what's left. Blame the style on the era; Blame the pettiness on conventional philosophy in the 18th century; Blame the constant hypocritical apology for sin on the censors, and then, take what's left in the book and cherish it — for it is called a great book. But what's left?

In appraising — praising — the book wise men choose this passage:

"As soon as he was gone, and I had shut the door, I threw off my hood, and bursting out into tears, 'My dear,' says I, 'do you not know me?' He turned pale, and stood speechless, like one thunder-struck, and not able to conquer the surprise, said no more but this, 'Let me sit down'; and sitting down by the table, and leaning his head on his hand, fixed his eyes on the ground as one stupid. I cried so vehemently, on the other hand, that it was a good while ere I could speak any more; but after I had given some vent to my passion by tears, I repeated the same words, 'My dear, do you not know me?' At which he answered, Yes, and said no more for a good while.'"

Sure that's good. Fine. But in the next paragraph the author, resting after having outdone himself, throws off the power of this scene by making the man (the Lancashire husband) suddenly fall passionately in love with Moll — his none too chaste wife — age 65 already yet, with cracks on her kisser and sunken eyes from prison life. Real sex appeal, she's got. At 55 she manages to seduce a nobleman. OK she's got it! Now at 65 —— pugh! Victorianism I like. Modernism I like. Swift I like. But just between me and this line, Defoe is a clever fool. What Fielding would sneeringly call a GREAT man. — And like that GREATEST of GREAT men of GREATNESS, Jonny Wild, I'd like to see Daniel "hanged by the neck till he was dead" for the time he wasted messing up the good parts of his books.

Just for fun I think I'll burlesque the passage I quoted. (Remember, Moll is 65, her spouse 60 — but well preserved. Moll is a withered wreck.) (note good use of sentementalism!)

"My dear," croaks I, "do yo not know me?" He turned pale, and started retching, like one thunderstruck in the belly, and not able to conquer his odorous vomiting, said no more

When when Poya ate his dragout & brown over his wit. Byzantia (according to Edgar Johnson)

but this, "Let me sit down!" and sitting down by a table, he laid his elbow upon his plate of beans and potatoes, and hanging his chin off his hand, fixed his eyes on his nose as one stupid. I cried so vehemently, on the other hand, that it was a good while ere I could speak anymore; but after I had given some vent to my amourous passion (for 65 is not as old as you think) I stopped crying and let him go, saying, "My dear, do you not know me?" At which he puked some more and answered, "Glurgle", and said no more for a good while.

Oh mother! Don't I write pretty prose!?

Last night after coming home from a practice for the Monon audition the Goose and I climbed the brick wall of Locust Manor, crawled through the 2nd story window of Walt Black's room, and pushed a dresser against a door so that he couldn't get in.

An hour later he and Bob Price brought to us — very formally, without comment — this note:

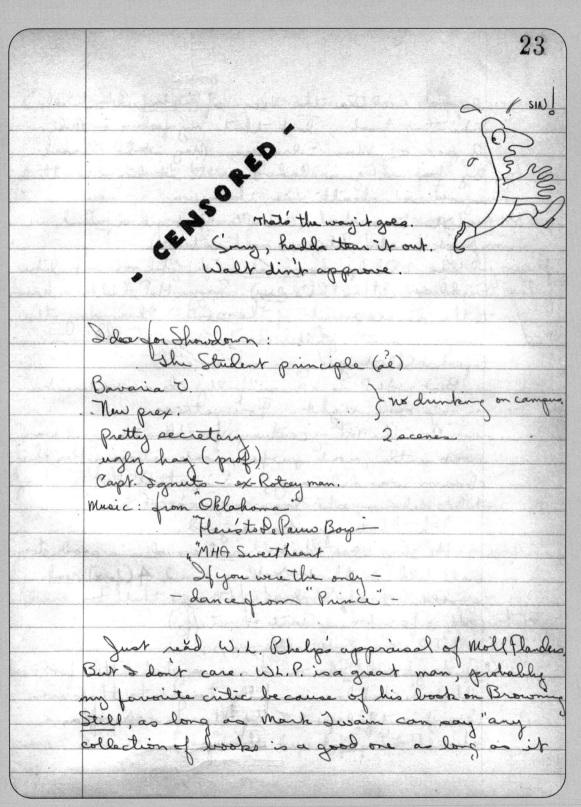

- CENSORED -

SIN!

That's the way it goes.
S'rry, hadda tear it out.
Walt din't approve.

Idea for Showdown :
       The Student principle (a?)
Bavaria U.
New prex.   } no drinking on campus.
Pretty secretary   2 scenes
ugly hag (prof)
Capt. Ignuts - ex-Rotcey man.
Music : from "Oklahoma"
            Here's to DePauw Boys -
         "MHA Sweetheart
          If you were the only -
         - dance from "Prince" -

    Just read W. L. Phelp's appraisal of Moll Flanders,
But I don't care. W.L.P. is a great man, probably
my favorite critic because of his book on Browning.
Still, as long as Mark Twain can say "any
collection of books is a good one a long as it

doesn't include the Vicar of Wakefield." Well, I
like that book, but that's my feeling on Moll.
A pox on Mrs. Flanders. May it be cursed
by future generations until it dies an utterly
ignominious death. So there.

(It's two am — Oct 10 — but never mind, we
won't make this a new entry.)

Wm. L Phelps is great. Oh, he doesn't like
Fielding either. (I do.) Says "H.F. did more harm
to the development of the novel than any other
single monster" [with a pen.] To me, Fielding's
tops. So it goes.

But WLP is an awfully clever satirist
in his own right. Forinstance:

"Now the 18th — century fashionable girl was
most gentle, most proper, most retiring. Her chief
charm was delicacy; and if she had a touch of
tuberculosis, she became irresistible."

Oh that's great and good.

He says also that a real novel is "a good story
well told. I think I have read 4 (four) real
novels. 2 by Dickens. (Maybe that's too cruel.)
(no, I forgot Jane Austin's stuff.)

WLP also, satirically, says:
"* [passages like] "on one occasion her little foot moved
'atho' she had been carefully taught to that even
this beautiful portion of the female frame
should be quiet and ~~unruly~~ unobtrusive." Many

readers politely surmise that Cooper was an ass."

Me too.

Glanced thru Rabelais. The good Dr Johnson was no novelist. Great maybe (as Fielding looked on greatness) but as a novelist. A drip.

You know, this unguided reading of mine is bad, I fear. I just decide, all by myself that a guy is putrid (?). But I never really know. Ah me.

Goodbye sweet book.

This is the way the world ends

" " " " " " "

" " " " " " " .

Not with a bang but a whimper.

Oct 10 —

for Joan's paper in St. Louis Inst. of Music.

To you with wide eyes and blank address books
you who haven't flunked one yet
you who cringe beneath the white-
fanged soph'more
to you we dedicate this first issue.

You can see that I'm really a prose writer. I write verse with my left foot.

Oct 11 —

— THE LOVING FRIENDS —   — INCIDENT —

Ollie's boy

The Thompsons:

      Uncle Jim [Dead]

      Aunt Lill

      John — Grampa

      Anne — Gramma

      Dran — uncle

wives { Millie — Paul }   Ron — hired man, on tractor.
    { Louise — Peter } sons
    { Miriam — Don }
       ⌐ Bob ♂

Betty Lou — "baby" sister } naughty
Eddie — 7th Day

The girl at the piano.

   Jack }   , Sullen, naturalistic
   Paulie }   , two views
   Sally } kids   ₃ Good + bad mixed up
   Betty }   ₄ Burlesque in blues.
   Bobby }

2 collies

Lill: "It's so good to have one's friends around, times
like this." She meant it. Her sunken eyes were
too (tired) to support politeness.

   "Yes, It must be very nice," I said.

The Vision of St. Hilda.   Story
                    Terrible Irony
                "Sympathetic" approach.
Hilda ~~too~~ can't walk... musc. dyst?
Sees a vision, can, now (but doesn't bother.)
House? becomes shrine
∂2 statues. — Old priest teaches her Latin.
the people on the road.   Love story: handsome young
the doctor (protestant.)   man — needs help
                                in Latin. Boat
Pneumonia — Hilda dies.   ride.
        Sainted. Close with beauty of shrine [Box]
Contrast
Dialogue
Narrative
etc.;

Oct 12 —
        In the craft book Dr. Pence again and again   ?
begged the student to work hard, for his teacher's
time is valuable. Someday I will write a book
asking the prof to have some pity on the poor
student, who can't afford to waste hours listening to a
lot of conversational gaiety over stuff that's in the
book. The air would be quite profitably used on
bubble gum.
        This crime — boring the student — is especially
common in the ROTC department, but there it is

forgivable. The student is suffering in class instead of on the battle-field. However, our fine English department has traces of the practice.

For instance: 45 minutes in a course on Lit covered these subjects, as my notes show.

1. Various degrees, honors, robes, etc., bestowed upon students in some English and American colleges. (With a detailed account of how hot it was back in 19—.)

2. The school colors of Wooster, DePauw, Harvard, Yale, and some others. (I couldn't keep up, but hope to get my notes from a fellow next to me.)

3. Reasons why smoking will be permitted in this class, with a hurried history of the freedom here allowed.

4. The financial push by the Alums. This is it as I understand it. DPU wants money; a lot of it. (What if a depression hits — but of course, these are wise men, all wise men, and I have no right to comment) Well, the Alums must start a campaign to get themselves to give generously. Naturally to start a thing of this import the school must have a roarin' good party as a send off. But since no one but the Alums can afford it, they will finance the party that is supposed to put themselves in a mood to give drunkenly. Who but a college man could devise such a powerful plan. Irresistable, I call it.

5. If you see an important personage, run up to him and shake his hand. He wants to know

you. (That's not bad, but unfortunately, in polite society, this kind of action is generally considered the mark of an odd-ball. — Well, I betcha plenty of lovely chaps will take the good deity's advice and say, "Hello doctor. I am Percival Abbington Northhaughy the fourth, from Muncie, Ind. I am a Tau Kappa Epsilon, and plan to make a 3.00 average. I am a virgin. I never drink. Here, take one of my cards.")

6. See a REAL, LIVE Nobel Prize WINNER! FREE!! The only D.P.U. Nobel Prize WINNER in captivity!

7. Never forget a word one of these intellectual, outstanding, swell, real fine personages say. They sat up all last week thinking of it, and they know how to deliver it. Yeah man.

Then of course there's another prof in the Eng dept. Y'know, when I get big, daddy, I wanna be like professor Gigglebumps. An instructor of her rank and bearing has not only the priviledge of boring her students to distraction, but also of channeling full concentration upon the uninteresting subject at hand. Hence, the student cannot share his misery with a passing bird or spider or discorded senior running home
P.S. Dear teach. I'll get you, come showdown.
                            You WAIT!

SEE NEXT PAGE

(Oct - 13)

Dear me, page 30, you look cross. I'll bet you really believed all that stuff I wrote yesterday. Remember, from now on "Lies, Lies, Lies" and don't be hurt so easily. I swear, you're the tempermentalest paper I've ever written on. I use a naughty word and you sulk till I blot it out. I sound mad and you pout. All right, all right! I'm sorry. And besides I lost the Monon yesterday. You'd be mad too. Ya see, the guy who won, won last year. A good writer. But his book was only half finished, and his music just started. What I'd he had was so bad that the young judges got Bill, my partner, to rewrite it for him. Too bad, isn't it. I was rather pulling for John Jakes'. Bob Zemon's might have been an awful flop, but I thought it was funny. So did the judges. Alas, against the advice of the advisors, our girls picked John's.[1] For John is sparkling and bright. He better be brighter than last year. I'm sorry for the girls though. Somebody may find out they are all dating in John's frat house. They won't understand. They'll be nasty! But not I! I'm virtuousk!

Speaking of lies, "All the world loves a lover" is a lie, by gosh.

← Kupid.

[Before we go into this let me explain my method. I, when starting a discussion of this nature, love to choose the side which <u>seems</u> wrong but isn't. You see, I come from a long line of harrangues. Lawyers, preachers, philosophers, professors, and fish-mongers. Well, in developing my arguments I like to convince you that I'm dead wrong by using weak arguments, unnecessary sarcasm, and bad illustrations. Then, after pages of this, I come to one sensible argument. Sometimes I forget that one by the time I reach it, but I don't care who wins. It's the joy of jousting I'm out for.]

I'm a normal fellow, and lovers disgust me. In life, of course, they're too ridiculous to have any place in a work of this paper's intellectual caliber. But even in literature I can't stan' em. I, personally, am madly in love with a sweet li'l red-head. She is the finest girl in the world, and I'm marrying her in June. But if you are sensible, you'll laugh at me, just as I would at you. Behold my case a moment longer. Me, I'm so thin and delicate that a dischord between

two tricycle horns could transform my
body mass to a weak electrical impulse.
Joan outweighs me by ten pounds, at least.
Me, I can't remember my way back to Locust
from the union building, I'm that dull. Joan
is finishing both S.I.M. and W.V. in a year.
Looking at it sensibly, isn't it crazy? But
I like the girl.

Now look at literature. Name your lover
and I'll laugh at her. (Don't name Romeo +
Juliet though. Joolie was only 13, as I recall,
And I'm not sure she knew what was coming
off.)

Of course there are Grace Livington Hill
characters like Seagrave and Emily (who reek
with purity). '"Seagrave, dear" she said,
venturing to touch his smooth white hand.' I'm
in hysterics already.

Or there's Steinbeck, where he and she (forgot
the names) enjoy each other on a dead woman's
cold corpse. (Course Steinbeck wants you to
be a little disgusted, methinks.

And there's the Saturday evening Post.
I'm getting tired of this. But note how
seldom you believe a guy will really love-till
death his gal when he swears he will. I guess
only a lover loves a lover, and even then, I
laugh at everybody but me. Gad I'm a
disgusting cuss!! ← ya can do that in a journal.

I'm ashamed of myself. All this vulgar talk in such a nice book! I'll buy a new pen and balance this trash with good. But first, "one lowest fling!"

Eve, she was a merry soul,*
And so was Adam, on the whole.
Gad, I can't stand it. I can not look at such sinful rot. ∴ I'll turn to a new page.

* Writ by Hal Peterson for our "Back to <u>Natural</u> ism" campaign. (No drinking, no swearing, no smoking. Just sex.)

Oct 23, 1952 — Thursday.

Henry Fielding was a great guy.
Phelps says he slowed down the
progress of the novel by advocating
digressions at the beginning of each
book in a work. Me, I wish novelists
would do it some more. Those digressions
dont in the least tempt me to skip.
They build suspense, and at the same
time please me with their thoughtfulness. His books become one long (886
pages for Tom Jones) essay. Never, at
any time does the author leave the
stage. He becomes a sage with a
$3 seat making clever comments as
the play progresses. Reading Fielding
is like going to a good play with
someone who knows it well. Between
the acts we have delicious commentary
on the thing. It's great! I swear, if
I can ever become a writer (and I can't
because I like this sort of thing) I
shall — when my fame is established —
take up the style of Fielding.

George Saintsbury, or some equally
tiresome critic, once said that
"when novelists realized the importance

of what they were doing, they stepped away from the lights and let their characters take over. In other words, men like Fielding were just playing around, and accidentally started the literary ball rolling. By George, t'ain't so. Fielding, I think, must have been pretty doggone serious about his work. And what he has to say is, to him, and to me, as important as anything later novelists wrote. He had, furthermore, a more serviceable(?) tool than those writers had. While they must put all their ideas into the mouths of characters – a limitation which brought about many of the long, dull soliloquies (?) found in later (and earlier) works — Fielding could keep his characters human, and now and then step in to say a few words himself.

Other critics have said that Fielding was too intellectual, too cold, to write convincingly of love. Oh was he? I'll not copy here the passage from Tom Jones wherein Tom finds Sophia with a bloody nose (inflicted by her pa) and they share their beautiful sorrows – but there is no more touching scene in Goldsmith, or, for that matter, in Jane

Austin.

Gad, I sound like a school boy who has just discovered The Little Prince. Well, I don't care. Fielding is not as bad as they say.

And neither is Mickey Spillane. By god, the man is gifted! Compared to Trollip(?) or, for my money, Defoe (now there's a rash statement) he's a genius. Mickey boy can describe. Mickey boy can tell a story. (Granted, you've heard the story before.) If Mickey Spittoon has any fault, it is that he writes the wrong kind of book, for the wrong kind of publisher. Cloth binding would make Spillane a "great American author." 1.) He writes romances. His villans are all bad, or nearly. 2.) He writes the kind of book that we're not supposed to have any more. "purpose novels", or books to teach a lesson. Fielding did it — but now days we realize that problems are too big to be answered in one book — especially a book of modern novel length. So he's wrong there. But there are such books. (New Wives for Old, is one, I think) I've never heard anybody who has read a Spillane book criticize it as I have here. That is to say, only those who have heard about him laugh at 'im. Correction: "Great" critics call him pulp. (The same "great" critics called *The Naked & the Dead* the "greatest story to come out of the war." Bull, I say. Anyway, Mickey is not so bad. As someone has said, he's "The highest of the lowest." To me, that's higher than the lowest of the highest.

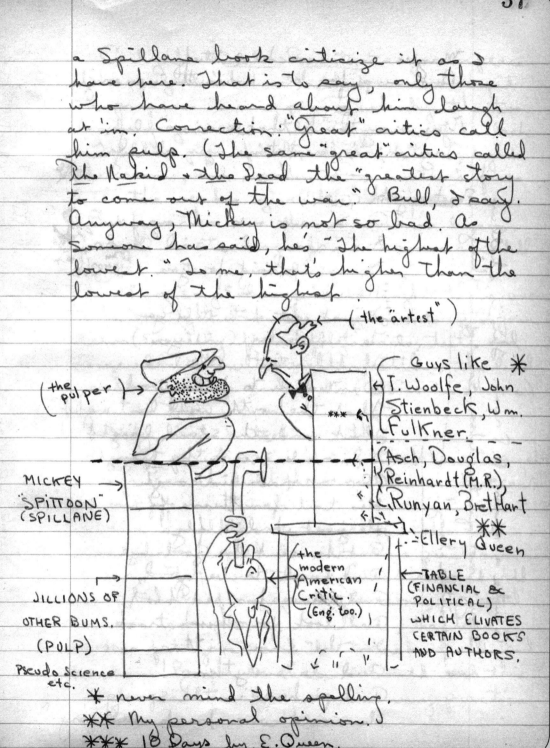

(the "artest")

(the pulper) →

Guys like ✳
T. Woolfe, John
Stienbeck, Wm.
Fulkner.

✳✳✳ ↞

Asch, Douglas,
Reinhardt (M.R.),
Runyan, Bret Hart

MICKEY
"SPITTOON"
(SPILLANE)

✳✳
Ellery Queen

the
modern
American
Critic.
(Eng. too.)

JILLIONS OF
OTHER BUMS.
(PULP)

Pseudo Science
etc.

← TABLE
(FINANCIAL &
POLITICAL)
WHICH ELIVATES
CERTAIN BOOKS
AND AUTHORS.

✳ never mind the spelling.
✳✳ My personal opinion.
✳✳✳ *10 Days* by. E. Queen.

Maybe sex is wicked stuff
But weep for him who's had enough.

You may think that sex is silly;
Try it, sis, next time yer chilly.

———o○o———

Frost sayeth (saith!)

As I went out a Crow
In a low voice said "Oh
I was looking for you
How do you do?
I just came to tell you
To tell Lesley (will you?)
That her little Bluebird
Wanted me to bring word
That the north wind last night
That made the stars bright
And made ice on the trough
Almost made him cough
His tail feathers off.
He just had to fly!
But he sent her good-bye
And said to be good,
And wear her red hood,
And look for skunk tracks
In the snow with an axe—
And do everything!
And perhaps in the spring
He would come back and sing."

(left margin, rotated) Is he a man? R. Frost. This is, shall we say, not quite like some of his things. Veritable hog!

54

Carlyle in <u>Sartor Resartus</u> says someplace (I've forgotten where) that war is stupid. He proposes a new plan whereby the two leading generals will "in person, take each a Tobacco pipe filled with brimstone; light the same, and smoke in one another's faces till the weaker gives in;" ~~but of~~

But from this man has learned no lesson. Carlyle wrote long ago, and wars are still our #1 international sport.

Fielding says men should fight their wars with naught but the implements god gave them, namely fists, fingernails, teeth and tongues. Then, after the battle, the dead could rise up and walk (albeit in shame) home to their women.

Nobody lissent to him either.

Funny peculiar, isn't it, that we universally agree with both these gentlemen but can't get out of our trench.

On a small scale sending bibles and missionaries would be silly as a preclusion of war. Yet even the hardest jingoist will agree that if we spent the money we spend on war on plows, teachers, tractors, bibles, fertilizers, and How to make friends and Influence People books we could end this idiotic strife. Man isn't a very practical creature.

If you tell me that I can do my math in ½ the time with your new slide rule, and prove it to me, I'll thank you from the bottom of my heart, buy your gadget, and, in all probability put the thing in a drawer — or sell it for 25¢ more than it cost me. So it goes. T.S. Eliot would fit in here nicely, but I'm going to bed. G'nite sweet page (as Oscar Wilde would say.)

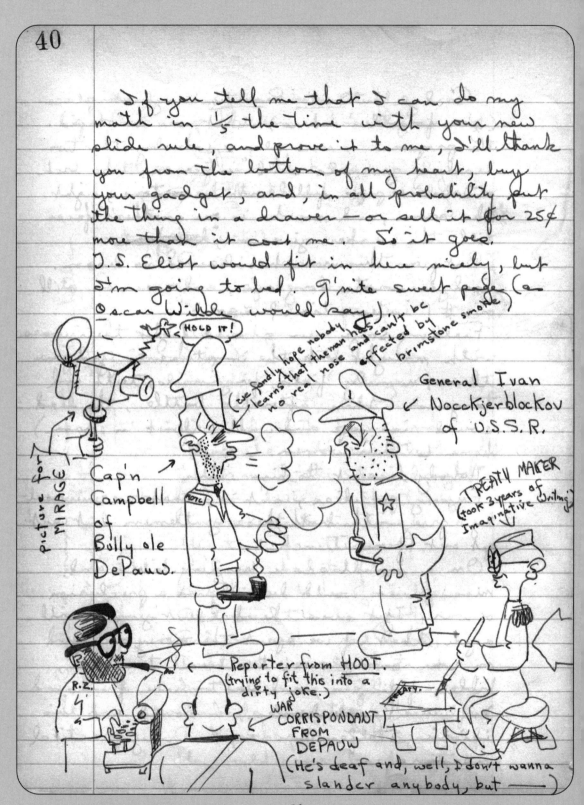

HOLD IT!

picture for MIRAGE

Cap'n Campbell of Bully ole DePauw.

(we fondly hope nobody learns that the man has no real nose and can't be affected by brimstone smoke.)

General Ivan Nocckjerblockov of U.S.S.R.

TREATY MAKER (took 3 years of Imaginative Writing)

R.Z.

Reporter from HOOT. (trying to fit this into a dirty joke.)

WAR CORRISPONDANT FROM DePAUW (He's deaf and, well, I don't wanna slander anybody, but ——)

TREATY.

Oct 27 - 52

One grows tired of little thoughts, after a while, just as one grows tired of laughing. And yet there are no big thoughts. There are only memories, pictures of people who could have big thoughts. Dad — Mr Reson — Little kids not old enough to know that it's all a big joke. There are serious places — like thin spots on an old old shirt. But pull on a new checked jacket. Hide the frayed edges. Laugh some more. There are no big thoughts for small minds — and yet, you can take the humor out of a little thought — look at it honestly — make it a little bigger. Like —

    Bird on a dead tree
     How come you sing
    Can a bird see
     — Long before me —
     Spring?

There are pictures, too. Thanks, god, for pictures. You can look at things and know that they have in them a big thought — only you can't quite catch it. Still you can look at it and know that there is a big thought there. There are stories — like Grapes of Wrath that imply big answers — but you can't quite catch 'em. Books like Of Mice & Men; like Clarissa,

MESSY AIN'T IT.

like, Darkness at Noon. Pictures — and
things outdoors. Like —
      Tamarack.
      There's power in the word, don't you think?
      Power in the word, as in the tree.
      Power from the thunder-bolt that fell
      And split it end for end last spring.
      Belly northward now it stands.
      Grim. Reared for war.
      Sixty long-haired arms stretched out
      Patient, sullen.
      Waiting for the storm.

Oct 31 or so. I can't keep track of insignificant details.

A mood is with me. I have lots of
interesting moods; but this one has been
with me so much of late that I can't
clearly remember the faces of the other ones.
This mood has stepped out of me, become
more real than myself. He sits over there
in my chair reading Clarissa and chain
smoking my cigarettes. The book is propped
in his lap — his feet are on my bookcase —
and with a free hand he teases the blotches
on his face.

Now and then he glances up at me
with a smile that may be meant to mock.
"Whatter you laughing at?" I say, and he
grins wide and says "something I read," and
he looks at me cornerwise so I know he's
lying.

It's queer — sitting here looking at a
mood. Sitting in one corner of a room looking
at a part of yourself that has stepped out
and taken life for itself. He blows smoke
at the page. It bounces, spreads out, out
until it is air. He exhales again, and sucks
the white cloud back through his nose. And
I would like a cigarette but I have none.
I am over here without cigarettes; maybe I

haven't even life. It seems as though I've given up to the mood. Given it my name, my chair, my book, my life, my cigarettes.

The mood is laziness; or no, cleverness. I don't know what it is. But it's mighty convincing. It tells me I'm a fool, and more than that, college is a national lie. Our fine land abounds with wretches who have been to college. But they know nothing. I have here a pile of good books. Some of them I've read. I know that if I could read those books I would be wise. All wise. I have an idea about satire. I know that if I were given one year, I could write a book on satire in the English Novel, 1704 – 1900; a book that has never been written; a book that must be written someday, for all critical studies of the English novel must be based on a good knowledge of my subject. The whole evolution of the novel rests on the genius of satire. Satire was the sperm that brought Mme. Epic her incomparable infant, the novel. I have it all organized. But I must read and read and read. I can't, you know. I have to go to Chemistry for five hours each week to do a few score experiments, every one of which I can already explain all phases of

procedure ± result. I must stand for
five horribly dull hours each week
studying something I already have
studied, so that I can get university
credit & dear, precious stuff. I must
spend fifty[1] minutes per week standing
in my shorts learning how to exercise
and "keep fit". This when I could be
reading good stories from Balzac (which
I haven't, in two years found time to
read) or putting into practice what
I've picked up out of the latter chapters
of a craft book by Uzzle.

 That mood is leering again. What
would you have me do, mood? I can't
flunk out. It would be silly. And yet,
to pass everything is to bow to the "hurry-
thru-this — just-so-you-can-pass-the-test"
boys. I don't want your slimy degrees.
I want stuff I can use when I want
to write. You won't make a Koch out of me,
so why this nonsense. While you stand
over me commenting on my sloppy lab.
procedure, Guillian Le Bel is inventing
penicillin — a new, cheaper, wonder
drug. All departments standardize

[1] (25 min. per day, counting dressing time)

their courses for the good + the poor,
the major + the minor. But these
things are all <u>little</u> difficulties. The
important thing is, I haven't any cigarette.

— I'm sorry that DePauwites in general
are so clever. I'd write this as a satire,
but I'm tired and too much satire, even
my own, nauseates me. The play tonight was not very good. I admit it. The
actors all missed the boat, probably.
But the student critics missed it by
a far greater margin. I went with two
very fine fellows — intellectuals, for whom
I have nothing but respect. Really. But
at the end of the second act they left,
and, ever since, they have been laughing
at the "putrid production." I have been to
plenty of plays — amateur and professional.
I am sorry that a good play must get
its laughs from sex and drunkenness, but
<u>still</u> I don't like the hi brow criticisms
I have to sit through when it's all over.
It is an acknowledged fact, no doubt,
that one cannot criticise a play unless
he knows a great deal about dramatics.
So he who finds nothing but fault must
indeed be a very clever critic. I'm guilty

too, I know. Seldom can I sit through a French horn recital. I know French horn. I'm a damn good cornist. I won't apologize. So I find fault, and in so doing become an example of what I have said here. You gotta know your subject to criticise it. But it seems to me an awful lot of the dramatic critics floating around this campus — floating - it's no cliché here. They're really up there — a lot of 'em don't know beans. And to sound like they do, they must criticise. Now I say that the third scene of tonight's play was damn well written. Those lines didn't _need_ an actor behind them. True, they didn't have one. But when I speak of the play I speak of the lines and "accidentally" omit mention of the actors. The lines left me teary, and by george I'm no sentimental bastard. It was a good play. The prologue was too long — that is, the first two acts — but the play was good. Hell with the acting. The kids aren't actors. Face it. I feel sorry for the guys who left before the play - that is - the ~~first two~~ third ~~scene~~ act - started. And I'm still sorrier for the schmucks who noticed the ham that flavored those good lines. I'm sorry for the recognized "great writers" who said the lines were a "prostitution of art — merely stuck on as tear jerkers. For the love of Mike, man, did Clarissa die to make the story sell better? Did Hamlet? Did Mr. Bramble go mad so that I would read the book? Did Medea kill her kids so the tickets could be sold for more? How 'bout Anna Karanina? or Raskolnikov? Don't feed me that spinach about lines stuck in to sell the play. I won't eat. I'll retch. (This is getting violent; dear, dear.) I like to hear a good critic speak. I hate to listen to intellectual hypocrites. And usually I manage to forget even what our good critic said. I never read reviews. They bore me. Make me tired as the devil in a WCTU meeting. (Although that good gentleman must be commended for the good work he does there in spite of the ladies' good intentions.) I admit it, I almost left early. But I didn't. Hooray for me. So much for you, noble critics.

pooo!

Afterthought (Long after): What would this have been like if I waited for it to cool? Obviously in anything but a journal, I'd have to.

Nov 5th

'As for the motto ... I desire that it
may not be engraved in the Greek and
Latin lingoes ... but in plain English, that
when the angel comes to pipe all hands
at the great day, he may know that I
am a British man, and speak to me in
my mother tongue.' — Smollett

Nov 6 —

Here I go, making another dull and trite
observation. But no matter how often a
phenominan has been observed in the past, it is
always worthwhile to observe it again. Otherwise,
why do we have elementary chemistry, or
sermons 52 Sundays a year?

If a society were completely happy it would
be completely stupid. That is, completely witless,
dull mentally, — without understanding. For when
we are happy we just can't think. Period.
We float on our joy and any serious thought
is beneath us. The men who make great advances,
the men who make sage observations, are
the suffering Carlyles: the rhumatic Mathiew
Brambles: The oppressed Dostiefskis: the
hypochondriactic Johnsons. A happy, (with
a child-like happiness) serene fellows have
nothing to say. Their only mode of expression

is a sigh — and who can sit down for an hour and converse with a sigh? Grace Livingston Hill was exultant in her religious joy. Her books show it. Her chapters are happy sighs that show a feeling, but, in analysis, contain little more than happily exhaled air. Kathrine Mansfield, on the other hand, has a sound, intellectual religion, not based on white clouds and yellow flowers, but on a racking cough, a headache, blood in the throat.

I have been trying all day to study, but I'll be damned if I can. (It's warm outside; my girl loves me; Dad sent $5; I got an A on a theme; Pence called me "discerning"; I got a paper published.) I can see that Humphrey Clinker has certainly got it rough, but I don't much care. I can see that Swift is right, we're all bastards, but I kinda enjoy it. I can see that there can be no afterlife, as Koestler maintains, but I still look forward to it.

Now you may think that this is just observation, and stupider than the society I talked of in the beginning. Well, if I left it at observation, it would be awful, rotten, retched writing. So what is the practical application?

Well, in the first place, we can build

our world on it. That's a very impressive application. And, I might say, a popular one thru the ages, for every observation of a philosophical nature. We can have the most supremely intellectual society in the history of the world. How?

1. Inflict pain upon everybody. Raise taxes, outlaw dirty jokes; Raise the comp. education limit to 35. etc. Make em unhappy; for from dissatisfaction + sorrow comes thought.

2. Revise the educational system. (The object of the present one is, it seems to me, give 'em a good time.) Make the prime objective a souring of soul which will result in works of genius to outshine Dante's Inferno, Carlyle's bitterest books, Swift himself.

3. Save time. Cut out the sabboth by cutting out religion which gives pleasure. Then, since there are 265,257 days in an astronomical year we will give philosophers and mathematicians great sorrow in trying to divide that number by six. People will die of overwork, which will inflict more sorrow (they get no vacations on Sunday.)

Now I'll tell you a secret. I have proved my original point. You can't think sensibly when you happy. Unfortunately, I'm happy. It's a horrible feeling, but, I hope, it has almost left me.

Nov. 8th

Last year Crandall said that the primary difference between man and monkey is the homo sapiens' thumb. He said that a child was raised with an exactly the same age monkey. They developed at the same rate until the thumb got in the way. The monkey couldn't create with blocks or crayons (etc) because he couldn't grasp things. He hadda scoop 'em. Well, suppose that an extremely intelligent ape were given (by medical means) a human thumb. Suppose he developed as a man. — Great fictional possibilities, eh? The doctor treats the ape as a son — etc. etc. —— But at last the ape falls in love with a human female. Great eh? Ha ha!

————— oOo ——

Nov 13

Here's a note to you who speak or write:
Verbosity's a thing you've got to fight.
Shakespeare saith of lecturers + such
"Me thinks my laddie doth express too much.

20 November 52

    I hate William Makepeace Thackeray with a beautiful, blooddripping hate. And I think R.W. Pence is an inferior Lit teacher. (Which has no connection except that both men are damn egoists.) What did Thackeray ever do that had any good use whatsoever? He developed an idea about how books should be written, and by whom (meaning fine men of the upper class — like himself); and proceeded to write Vanity Fair, Henry Esmond, and a batch of other stupid[1] novels. Then, still

---

1. No slight meant here. They may be very nice novels in most respects. But to me they are tripe. Charming, moving, interesting — maybe, but mostly just stoopid.

---

hunting for a field in which to show his talents he took up slandering greater authors than himself. A critic ∨ an angry author who lives in a house made of reject slips, or else a vain bastard who'll do anything to make an appearance before his dear public. Once in awhile — one or two per century — a real scholar honestly turns adventurer and names himself a critic. (Saintsbury)

(left margin, vertical:) G.K. Chesterton is one of these — she only had his pull on Browning — but that is utter rot.

I don't know which of these Thackeray was, but he certainly had the fingernails for the job! I hate iz guts, I do. And because W.M.T. dislikes them, I love Sterne and Swift, and guys like that. Thackery is one of the most vulgar, nauseus, cruel, inhuman, slanderous, simple-minded, malevolent, malignant, morbid, caustic, ill-informed, opinionated, dogmatic, de-based, impolite, and egotistic Yahoos that ever lived. He says of Swift:

"Would you have liked to be a friend of the great Dean?...If you had been his inferior in parts... his equal in mere social station, he would have bullied, scorned, and insulted you; if, undeterred by his great reputation, you had met him like a man, he would have quailed before you, and not had the pluck to reply, and gone home, and years later written a foul epigram about you — watched for you in a sewer, and come out to assail you with a coward's blow and a dirty bludgeon." That's about all the ink I can spend on that kind of (I need a word here. Something like dung but more polite - more cutting.)....

Since I have not the stomach to go on and copy more (though all of Thackeray's

essay on Swift is like this — demoniacal)
let me analyze the sneakiness, the petty
hatefulness in W.M.T.

The part about — he would have bullied, scorned,
insulted you. This is ridiculous. Swift was
noted for his genius at making friends of
both sexes. So W.M.T. disregards this fact
and attacks one or two isolated incidents
found in Swift's biographies — The Earl of Orrery,
Scott, Sheridan, Johnson — everybody that
wrote was so perplexed by a few of Swift's
most cutting satires that the biographies changed
their whole mood. Swift's light repartée was
twisted and given ominous significance —
even called madness in the 19th century.
And all these things Thackeray pounced
upon, blew up, until he could say "— as if
the wretch who lay under that stone awaiting
God's judgment had a right to be angry."
To Thackeray I say in the words of Grenidin
etching "I spit in the milk of your grandmother."

When Defoe aimed his Thackeray-like blasts
at "the learned Dr S——" the good Dean didn't
even bother to answer — that's how misanthropic
he was on a personal scale. Then when he
wanted to defend a later work he remembered
the dig and casually mentioned the "fellow
who was pilloried." This, I take it, is the

"foul epigram" W.M.T. speaks of. Or no, since Defoe was a lower-class man it must have been someone else. But the principle is the same. Ah well.

Education and learning are enemies of one another. The above tirade is an example of this. [By education I mean the passing of tests etc. which win a man the epithet "scholar." Learning I consider the acquirement of knowledge.] Now in a lit course none of this information [1] is of any particular value.

---

1 (The above tirade)

One must know dates, facts, statistics. Obviously, the more time spent in memorizing facts, the less time left for mere research. (That's why spelling is a crime. Students spend the best years of their lives learning to spell instead of thinking and exploring so that they have something to say with the words that they can spell.) Our system of education not only absorbs so much of the student's time that he can't stop to discover anything, but it actually encourages him to forget about thinking and spend his time memorizing. This fallacy

has sundry ramifications; politics are
ill founded; politicians are accepted on
faith; old ideas — like the physical
electrical current that goes the wrong
way — last' centuries after they've been
disproved. Religion, which is inclined to
be dogmatic, makes no advances, unless
there are advances backward.

But I digress even more than one should
in a half-assed book like this. I started
this present discussion to lead up to my
ideas of <u>Gulliver</u>, which I can't work into
any real school work cause I'm so darn
radical. Rather I must know that
Gulliver was written in 1718 — 1720,*
published in 1726, corrected in 1727,
and again in the 3rd edition (Faulkner's first)
in 1728; first standered in September 1726
by (I forget the name) a pamphlet that Johnson
got a hold of and made into his commentary on
Swift. Down with such rot!

Because I have a natural love for
argumentation, and because it is the popular
20th century mode to defend the slandered
author and scratch the exaulted, I immediately
started hunting up defences for Swift.
There are surprisingly numerous defences
* after the Tory fall of 1714 when Swift was
pushed back to Ireland.

possible. I say that Swift was a nice guy. The fourth book of Gulliver which slams mankind, I explain by saying, Swift was a preacher, a cleric, a divine. It is not the business of such a man to commend society. It is his duty to point out its failings. (This is a matter of self-preservation, for if clerics admit man is fine they have no reason to offer Redemption, so there.) So now an analysis of Gulliver as a lay reader (me) sees it, without all the trenchant wit, the ironic stink, the derogatory nonsense:

Say I: In Gulliver's Travels there are four books, and three distinct satirical aims. Books I and II, Gulliver's journeys to Lilliput and Brobdingnag, satirize government from two points of view. Book III, the trip to Laputa, etc., satirizes education and knowledge. Book IV, the trip to Houyhnhnmland points out human failings.

In Lilliput Lemual Gulliver was ~~thus~~ nearly thirteen times as tall as the king (a giant ~~who was~~ himself, almost a fingernail width taller than ~~his~~ tallest ~~subject~~!) From this great height it was easy to see the whole scheme of Lilliputan life and politics. The philosophical, political, and social question of how to break an egg, while it seems vital to the Lilliputan

appears to Gulliver in its true ridiculous
light. The selfishness of princes; the
prudishness carried to extremes, seen in
the result of Gulliver's philanthropic
battle with the palace fire; the
duplicity of courts; the misconceived
egoism of the tiny lords all show up
plainly to the omniscient mountain-top
eye.

Swift's irony flows continually, as
Saintsbury has said, but let us note
a few of his brilliant thrusts.
When first the "tall" monarch appeared,
Gulliver notes that: "He held his sword
drawn in his hand, to defend himself,
if I should happen to break loose;" (italics
mine.) "it was almost three inches long,..."
What a beautiful, tragic, hilarious picture of
man, proud, vainglorious!

A little later Gulliver witnesses a competition
for a vacated office in the Lilliputan Royal Court.
Gulliver says:
    "— five or six ... candidates petition the
    Emperor to entertain his Majesty and the
    court with a dance on the rope; and
    whoever jumps the highest without
    falling, succeeds in the office. Very

often the chief ministers themselves are
commanded to show their skill, and to
convince the Emperor that they have not
lost their faculty. Flimnap, the Treasurer, is
allowed to cut a caper on a straight rope, at
least an inch higher than any other lord
in the whole empire. I have seen him do the
Summerset several times together upon a
trencher fixed on the rope, which is no
thicker than a common pack thread in
England."

Note also the delicious satire in the
discussion of the three fine silken threads
a blue, a red, and a green, conferred as a
favor by the Emperor.

Then there's the episode of the monarch's
insatiable greed for more ships after
Gulliver has captured 60 longboats.

But I must hurry. I have my French
to do. (Education vs. Learning again.)

In the second book Gulliver gets the
opposite point of view. The Brobdingnagians,
60' tall are seen in exact detail. Perfumes
are so strong that Gulliver faints beneath
them. Here, through irony, he points
out the littleness, the pettiness of
his own type government & reasoning
compared to theirs. These two books,

then, attack government, primarily.

The Laputans, with their love of ~~Math + ~~ science & music; their intolerance of the old in their search for new, glorious truth; their absorbtion in thought (so great that they need rattles for conversation) which produces nothing — all these blast English study and ridiculous patronage of new new, new ideas, whether tried or not.

Now for Book IV: Critics say that — well, Orrery said, "Swift's misanthropy is intolerable. The representation which he has given us of human nature, must terrify, and even debase the mind of the reader who views it." Critics call swift a monster because he pointed out the sins of man. In one place Swift (or rather Gulliver) attacks man by saying that in Houyhnhnmland[?] "I did not feel the treachery or inconstancy of a friend, nor the injuries of a secret or open enemy. I had no occasion of bribing, flattering, or pimping to procure the favor of any great man or of his minion. I wanted no fence against fraud or oppression; here was neither physician to destroy my body, nor lawyer to ruin my fortune; no informer to watch my words and actions, or forge ac-

cusations against me for hire; here were no
gibers, censurers, backbiters, pickpockets,
highwaymen, house-breakers, attorneys,
bawds, buffoons, gamesters, politicians,
wits, splenetics, tedious talkers, controvertists,
ravishers, murderers, robbers, virtuosos;
no leaders or followers of party and
faction; no encouragers to vice, by
seducement or examples; no dungeon, axes,
gibbets, whipping-posts, or pillories; no
cheating shopkeepers or mechanics; no
pride, vanity, or affectation; no fops,
bullies, drunkards, strolling whores, or poxes;
no ranting, lewd, expensive wives; no stupid,
proud pedants (are you listening WMT?) "no
importunate, overbearing, quarrelsome, noisy,
roaring, empty, conceited, swearing companions; no scoundrels, raised from the
dust for the sake of their vices, or nobility
thrown into it on account of their virtues;
no lords, fiddlers, judges, or dancing-masters"
 The critics may scream that Swift has
painted a foul picture, call it "symptomatic
of mental disease," but they will not forget it;
and once in a while they will find themselves
doing something touched in that list. Will
they not be nauseated at a realization that
they are damnable Yahoos? Do not this

restraint due to
self-contempt higher than restraint as
a result of "Hell fire preaching"? Swift
does not ~~scold~~ bawl, like so many
divines about punishments in the next life;
he points his finger, frowns and administers punishment through concience
in _this_ one. Isn't he, then, a great
preacher? Call him insane. But there
is still an unpar_alleled_ scolding in
Book IV; and certainly no preacher ever
reached a wider audience than Swift.
John Wesley complained that it was, in his
day (he was a contemporary of Swift)
"quite out of fashion to suggest that
humanity [was] all wise, all innocent" etc.
  ∴. (And now I go to my French) Hail Swift!
and Hail with Thackeray, and all the
vampires that called out that noble vulture.

Nov. 29: - FRAGMENT -
      ...It is an evil night.
Fog lies writhing in the streets
...the green white soul of some huge monster,
Newly dead of poison.

Nov. 31: How stoopid ↑

December 9, 1952 yet still.
    I went to a party.
    It was an ordinary party, you might
say except for a few little things. It
was a birthday party but it was over
a month late because we who threw
the party happened to be broke when
Ben's birthday came. So nobody even
said "Happy birthday" on that real day.
Also it was held in a laundry. I
don't know that this is unusual, but
it was new to me. Madame Beaunet,
with whom Ben stays, is a connisseur
de handkerchief. She does fine cleaning
for fine (or at least rich) people. She
is not very well-to-do herself, so she
couldn't afford to fix up both her home
and her business. (Her husband died in
France in 1916, I think. There's a plaque
of medals with French words on 'em

hanging in Madam's living room - upstairs
from the laundry.) As I was saying,
since she's not rich herself, and must
cater (or rather prefers to cater) to the
upper set, she has put all her money
to the laundry. As a result that
part of the building is beautiful, with
a red red rug, a dazzling glass counter
and five or six huge, leather armchairs.
Hence, we had the party there instead
of upstairs. Another slightly unusual thing — It was a surprise
party, and Ben, who could not be
tricked into going down to the laundry
to be surprised was finally heaved down
the chute bodily. You should have
seen his jolly face when he phuglumphed
into the clothes pile to the tune of
Happy birthday to you.
      Ben and all of the party (except
myself who am divorced from such
things since I gave away my French
horn) were musicians of the first
oder. Ben had hardly disentangled
himself before the party began to
beat on Mario Lanza. By shorting a
steam iron Guy got his tape machine
to work and we put on bundles and on
the floor, and a few of us on the

cake my love tried to make, to hear
the horriblest of singers sing at
some lovely song.

I kind of liked it.

There was the Beethoven 9th as Toscanini
did it, too. This also I liked. There were
no conductors in the crowd, so we agreed
that the piece would do. Does this
sound dull and insignificant? Does this
bore you, make you sweat, make you
fidget and curl your lip?

I wondered if it would. Me to.

Been reading ~~Tory~~ Tristram Shandy.
Can't make sense of anything anymore.
I've discovered one thing, tho'. Life is
no use. Man hath no dignity. If he
likes a book he's dull, unoriginal,
sentimental, one of the crowd. This is
obviously true; but due (or thanks, if
you love your grammar) to mass education
everybody knows this truth; so everybody,
in order to avoid dullness, dissents. So
even dissention is dull.

→ This is such a small thought it
isn't worth condensing.

I have digressed a little, I'm afraid. I meant for this book to be a Locust Manor chronicle, but I kept slipping away into conversation and never getting to the point I've completely missed the one and only date nite we got here. A failure: the goose and Mr Getty plugged the chimney, and we're still finding hunks of pop-corn where the lovers left them in their flyte. And there was the mock murder, and the mirror-smash, and the war we had with the hi-school boys and the time Clapp came over and lost the tires off his car, and — alas! all this is old news now, and I've forgotten the details I meant to use (honestly or otherwise).

I meant to clip in the stuff I got published at Washington U, too — but there's still lots of time for that, I guess. I can't wait to see what I wrote for this issue's editorial.

Well, this didn't undigress me, but I feel reprimanded. Maybe I'll be better from now on.

CONFESSION OF A RAT.

WOOD KUT I have just read this thing up to hear, Lawse I'm a bitter one! Not really though. Life isn't half bad.

And next year in Wash. U. I'll have no friends, 'cept a wife, and I can study instead of help others thru. (More bitterness. Hafta watch that.)

MERMAID

Her eyes were warm. Beyond the sea the moon
was moaning as he rolled from May to June.
We saw the stars step back to let him through
and then slip close to get a better view.
~~Leuranna's breasts were warm against my skin~~
For we were on the shore, ~~Selina~~
and I.

(altho we knew) that one of us must
die...
Must die of love, for I, who
live in air
could not survive down in her ocean lair
And she, now paler than the moonlit
sand
could not live long upon the very land,
It's always been that way, and always will
I cannot love; to love would be to kill.
She slides into the sea. And in the sky
The moon is moaning — longing for July.

ottava rima   ON THINKING

a   Tired. Vague, unrelated things.
b   Mixed images, riding parallel.
a   First the fact. And then the fancy bringing
b   Dreams almost analogous, but which tell
a   Nothing. Always nothing. Murmurings.
b   Wisdom from a drooling imbecile.
c   Nothing, always nothing, murmurings.
c   Tired. Vague, unrelated things

Sometimes I almost think I have the ~~mean~~

Sometimes when I'm riding on a train

Ballad form

. I . I . I . I

. I . I . I

. I I I . I . I

. I . I . I

~ Atlantis ~

Not an unknown land, really
    The glorious, lost Atlantis.
Not a dead city lolling
    Between sunken mountains

And yet black, just the same
Abysmally black

○ / ◡ / ◡ / ◡ / ◡
　　　/ ◡ / ◡ / ◡

○ / ◡ / ◡ / ◡ / ◡
　　/ ◡◡ / ◡ / ◡

○ / (◡) / ◡ / ◡ / ◡ /
　　　/ ◡ / ◡◡ / ◡
　　/ (◡) / ◡ / ◡ /
　　/ ◡◡ / ◡ /

/ ◡ / ◡◡ / ◡
/ ◡◡ / ◡ / ◡ /

– Atlantis –

Crushed beneath the ~~awful~~ throbbing pressure
Of the sea, the city
~~Lay~~ On her ~~naked~~ belly, prostrate
Clings to a soggy mountain.

Streets — shifting, gloomy streets
~~that Roads~~ through yellowing seaweed.
~~Streets~~ Lined by frog-like ~~men~~ and cats
Whimpering to be fed,

Thick, slimy stone walls
Built ~~in another~~ for defense
Now decaying. ~~Open jells~~ Exposing cells
Where ~~once~~ rotted human souls
Dead long since.

Men ~~walk~~ wander through the city
Stir with the ~~moving~~ current
Move as God, the sea, may dictate
Walk the ocean floor.

They have no thoughts. Only dreams.
Dreams that lap at their brains
Saying "Rise, take up arms
Against ~~godless~~ pagan lands.

a   Then, like an ocean serpant

b   Rising from the muddy bottom

a   Eyes blazing, jaws snapping

a   Up to the surface ~~comes~~ Atlantis

a   Playing the national anthem.

The Human Hand,

ᴗ ι ᴗ / ᴗ ι ᴗ / ᴗ ι — / — ι ᴗ ι ᴗ ι —

ᴗ ι ι / ι ᴗ ᴗ / ᴗ ι ᴗ ι ᴗ ι —

ᴗ ᴗ ι / ι ᴗ ι ᴗ

A Journal—more or less—of John C. Gardner

"if it's worth telling, it's worth stretching."

(or in language of a senator, "Lies, villifications, filthy, slimy gossip!")

26 Sept. 52; Sunday

Read Katherine Mansfield's Journal today. Joan read over my shoulder. Maybe that book has told me how to keep this journal of mine. And how not to keep it. Most important in this thing, is sincerity, I guess. For instance, right now I have a doozey cold. I can record this fact in a number of ways. I can say—"26 Sept. 52—Have a hell of a cold," and go to bed. Or, "my red nose houses tonight a slithering half-formed serpent, whose tail whacks at the stellactites in my mind's chamber, while his head swells, as from his own foul venom, till my nostrils (mostly the right one—the left one only now and then) can scarcely contain him." Or, "Curse this ugly world. I have a cold. What joy is there in life? and what reward? A fie and a pox on this unguided, ungodded universe." Or, "I got a runny nose. Now, I know it's none of my affair; my nose is as old as I am and ought to know its business by this time; but it sure makes kissing awkward. Next time, friend nose, please choose to run when we're in Greencastle instead of here in St. Louis. Better still, take a tip from this year's presidential candidates and don't run at all till I ask you (and don't get yer hopes up, cause I won't—unless there's a Rotcey test I wanta miss.)"

Now if I sincerely feel any one of these, I'll write it. But at the moment I'd write nothing at all. I have no sentiments concerning the matter. The red nose simply exists.

I said before that I must be sincere. I didn't quite mean all that that might imply. After all, my joy is my dishonesty. I will be true to my mood—and I <u>am</u> a moody child. But as to facts . . . .

When I was younger I used to worry about my fibs. I thought I would surely burn for them one day. But now that I am older and have read Robert Browning and Mickey Spillane, I am not afraid. I consider lies life, and vice versa. How horribly dull would be a day on a tractor with no human within a mile, if one could not stretch the basic truths of his life to wild, yet believable, stories.

I used to frighten Bill—my mental and physical elder, with tales of how "Johnny Mills and me saw the ghost"—up in the overgrown, forgotten cemetery behind Kenny Lowell's.

I will say it's unfortunate that nobody can believe me anymore. Even Jack, the closest friend I've got (who else, of any sex, would meet me at 4 a.m. at a station one mile—on foot yet—out of town*. And me coming home from a most routine two-day trip. Greater love hath no man.) As I was saying, even Jack always gives me a chance to say I was joking when I tell him some silly, reasonless fib. But of course I always swear on my honor that they're true. Sometimes I swear to things that really <u>are</u> true. Life is very complex.

Still, I can be true to character in writing. I won't misrepresent anybody. But as to what they do—so, they can't remember it.

[Drawings]

29 – Sept. 52 – Monday

I must not leave my little roommate alone on weekends. It is not safe.

This weekend when I returned from St. Louis I found Locust Manor in a gentle uproar.

Right off the bat let it be understood that my boy Gooseberry (muh-roommate) never does anything naughty unless somebody else gives him the idea. Little Jackie <u>could</u> be very innocent.

---

* Roger Getty came too. Of this lad this book will hear more!

Harold A. Petersen is a house councellor in Locust Manor. Roger Getty is a sweet fella who never did anything more malicious than blow up a dietition's automobile (in 1951).

Said Harold A. Peterson to Roger Getty in the hearing of John Robert (Goose) Berry, "This place is too quiet."

Said Roger Getty, "Uh-huh."

Said Pete, "Somebody should short-sheet some beds, or take screws out of door-knobs, or something."

In the half hour that superceeded this delightful conversation, that is, while counsellor Petersen studied industriously, Mr. Getty and the Goose occupied them-selves with short-sheeting beds in the attic where we sleep, piling unused mattresses on the bed of one Wheel Barrow, polishing door handles with gobs of toothpaste (Colgate), owned by the Goose, and taking screws out of numerous door-knobs, in-cluding that which is attached to the public phone on the second floor of this noble building. For the information of this journal, a door-knob with the screw taken out will turn round and round in the hand of him who wants in, or out, making no im-pression upon the latch of the door.

Upon completing the numerous businesses mentioned above, Misters Getty and Berry went downstairs to push buzzers (which call the occupants of this our dormi-tory to the phone.) One by one, the boys came out, their hands dripping toothpaste, their angry mouths dripping foam. And profanity. Not to be left out, Misters Getty and Berry swore and dripped with the rest.

At bedtime, (close to midnight in this place) while Mr. Petersen slept, in came—

Mr. Z_____, who had just had a battle with the love of his life. Ready for tears, this lad. And, upon jumping into his sabotaged bed., ready to express more tangible emotion.

Mr. A _____, whose mottoe seems to be, "speak loudly while batting 'em down with yer big stick. (He batted down, among other innocents, Mr. Z_____, who lay softly cursing universal powers—like Mr. Clapp who should be on the job times like these.)

Wheel Barrow, who doesn't mind sleeping on six mattresses unless his pillow happens to be at the bottom of them. (A real princess, this.)

Mr. F_____, who saw the humor of it all. (He'd make a good frat man. He's cute.)

Mr. W_____, who immediately considered this a matter for the house council. (Not till morning tho!)

And so on, into the night.

At six a.m., when the last straggler came in (myself—just off the train), Mr. W_____, a light sleeper, had had enough.

"Pete," screeched he, shaking the sleeping bones of our councellor, "It's time we took some action!"

And so, at six-thirty, a very solemn house meeting was had by all. Unfortunately there are no minutes of this meeting, since our secretary is a heavy sleeper, even while sitting up in bed with a notebook in his hand.

"Fellow residents," droned Mr. Petersen, looking unhappily (and fruitlessly) for his pillow, "It has been brought to my attention that somebody has pulled a nasty. Now I happen to know the names of the instigators of this nonsense, and if that person, or those persons, will step forward at this time, no great harm will be done them."

(Peter didn't rise himself, so Getty and the Goose sat in their places.)

"Very well then we shall consider the matter closed." Upon which words Mr. Petersen lay back without his pillow.

Mr. W_____ had other ideas, which he voiced without timidity.

"Oh all right, " grumbled Pete after a brutal shaking. "If you think it that important I'll go to Kent and tell all."

Very patiently then our councellor went over and over the probable punishment and resultant unhappiness of all persons in the dorm until Mr. W____ said he was heartily sorry for his hasty indignation, and forgave the "harmless pranksters."

When the meeting broke up Mr. Berry found it necessary to telephone a friends to explain why he had missed his appointment with her at Monion (?) Springs.

At ten-thirty when I went by the telephone booth he was still there, looking very sad and bluish, making signs at the door-knob. I waved at him as I passed.

When I came in from classes at 3 p.m. I found the Goose <u>still</u> in the booth. (I don't know what went on between times, so I can't tell you.) On the window there was a sign reading:

> To whoever it may concern:
> Under normal conditions this is a public telephone booth, but due to the acute housing shortage the assholes of this university decided this should be a private room.

In there with him I saw (through much smoke) a box of candy (mine!), a pack of cigarettes, a notebook and some envelopes. Outside the door sat Mr. Getty, blowing the smoke of chloraphill cigarettes through the key-hole. Says Pete with great authority, "Quiet hours!" whenever Mr. Berry's screaming becomes audible through the panel. Says Mr. E. passing by, "That looks like a nice place. He should live about two days, anyway." And says Mr. Getty, "If there develops a shortage of air in there, don't breath so much."

That's all I know.

(To all this I solemnly swear.)

---

30 – Sept. 52 – Tuesday

Who put lighter fluid in the toilet bowls? Next time I'm gonna put my cigarette in an ash tray.

1 – October 52 – Wednesday

I begin to think this journal a good idea. I admit, at first I thought it a bit silly; but now I've changed my opinion. It is becoming a log of Locust Manor. In it I can record all the gay, crazy, friendly pranks—the serious thoughts—the strange, unbelievable close moments we have here. And I see that I was wrong in thinking that a good story is better when stretched.

[But then, I had other reasons for saying the stories were elongated. For one thing, protection. Nobody can be held responsible for crimes I have recorded (with no malicious intent toward the criminals) as long as I say, "oh, that was just a story." So I won't say these things are true. No, maybe they're not!]

Perhaps I ought to apologize to the whiteness of this page for useing some of the words I'll use—and have already used. But there is good humor in some of them, I think. Besides, this is a men's dorm. I'll not dress it to look like Gobin in April. No, by Joss.

This is getting ridiculous.

On September the 28th the Goose and I put a typewritten sign on our door:

GARDNER & BERRY ENTERPRISES.

That night a new sign decorated our port:

GARDNER & BERRY ENTERPRISES

PAY THE MADAM

On the 29th another new sign (on another typewriter, elite type):

GARDNER AND BERRY ENTERPRISES

ARE YOU SAVED?

On the 30th:

        GARDNER AND BERRY ENTERPRISES

        We ask all consultants: are you WORTH saving?

    Then tonight:

        GARDNER AND BERRY ENTERPRISES

        Will the sonovabitch who changed this sign please do it again?

    Somebody's naughty, I'd say.

[Drawing]

Someone should re-spell the dictionery. Everybody talks about it—Shaw for example, but we still have to follow the old. Some of us more closely than others.

The Monon script—The Serpent & the Dove—went in tonight. I like it. I just found out there's fifty bucks for the winning team. Now I'll worry. All I <u>really</u> hope is that Uncle Bobby's five night masterpiece doesn't beat out my twelve full months of concientious work. (What are full months? Cliché? Besides they're not full. Some are 28 days, some 31, and some have some other number, I understand. I don't pay much attention. It seems to me we oughtta start over. Yes, that's a good idea. What we need is a good war. I can say this, for I'm a phoole. Wiser men only approve war as a last resort. (spelling again. In the dictionary "resort" has to do with entertainment. end parenthasies.)

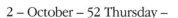

2 – October – 52 Thursday –

He's a good man. All wise, all sweet, all compassionate. His head bobs and his smile blooms like the head and smile of a bright-painted puppet in a wind tunnel. Or like a deaf-mute waiter trying to keep his job. He cocks his head and listens. Cocks it (click) like a batter waiting for a pitch. But in this case the baseball is not a baseball, but a gem out of the mouth of a suckling. (I'm he.) Don't you just love gems of wisdom Well, you ponder this one. Me, I'm going to bed.

— COLD TEA —

I can't understand this hot tea business.

"Dave, excuse me, but I wonder if you could run up and get me some hot tea? This is cold."

"Sure, ma'am. Be right with you."

"Hot, now. Not warm. Hot!"

"Yes'm."

She smiles at me. Her eyes glance down her nose, followed by the lids. You'd call it coy on a younger woman.

"That's the one thing about this place," she says. "The tea is never hot. I just can't stand cold tea."

"Neither can I," I say. I'm a conformist. A polite conversationalist. Crude people would say, "why can't you stand cold tea?" That's why they're crude, you know. They don't mind if the tea doesn't eat out their throats. But not I. I smile and say, "Neither can I."

Dave isn't there at all. A good waiter. His arm puts the cupful of steam in front of her.

"Oh thank you, David! Thank you!" She holds the seething stuff to her lips and sniffs it. "Oh that's good!" she says. Then she puts it down and waits for it to cool.

I sit and watch with half closed eyes and nearly casual eyebrows, like one of King Mythrandites' courtiers waiting for the soup to take its effect. I'm curious. But, as I say, not crude. My father told me all about sex, baseball, war, liquor—things like that. But he never said much about the peculiarities of nice society. He was a simple farmer. He didn't even know the seven rules for picking up crumpets. Well, I am out to learn, so I must watch.

I watch.

"Have you decided what you'll be when you graduate, John?" No move to the cup.

"I'm not sure, ma'am." (smile) "With the world situation what it is . . . ."

"Oh, I know!" (sigh.) Right hand dunks the tea-bag. In and out. In and out. A green ticket hooked to a white string - suddenly turning yellow about half way down. "No boy can plan anything these days."

"No ma'am."

"Will you be going to St. Louis again this week?"

"I think so. Jack too, if he gets his work done."

"That's nice." She's taking it now! In her hand! She drinks it—eyeing me corner-wise. I remember I'm staring. I look down. It doesn't matter. It's cold now.

And then I know that I am only a farmer, like my dad, and his dad, and his. One must be bred in society to understand it. Is it because a true blue-blood has a throat of tungston steel and must show it to all? No. The tea got cold. Was it because, in olden times, the master had to keep the servent busy?

"Is everyone finished?" She pushes back from the table. Bob, with a disinterested air, helps her rise. Cultured, that boy. But I don't know. I always used to kinda like some of the crude men and women who submitted, without thought, to cold tea. College is disillusioning, isn't it. All I can say is, I'm glad I'm young enough to learn new ways.

No thanks Clement. I can't take your cigarette. In the first place your not a frat man, and in the second, it hasn't got a filter. Third, what would I do with the Lucky I'm smoking?

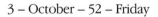

3 – October – 52 – Friday

Some day I must write a satire on Reader's Digest condensations. A three page book (profusely illustrated with those Mother Goose type illustrations common to that magazine) for busy readers who don't care what the writer <u>really</u> wanted to say. I'll maybe call it <u>The Can Mutiny</u>. Short sentences and fragments. Real ugly.

---

8 October – 1952 –

    I was just serenely in bed when the door sneaked open. In crept two black shadows. I could not see, in the darkness, who lived in the black hulks, but I had no fear, for there are none but sweet, gentle souls in Locust Manor.

    For a long time the shadows crouched at the foot of the bed next to mine— whispering and giggling. Then they became silent. I almost thought them worried. But I made no move, for I was dog-tired and needed my sleep. At length, one of the shadows moved foreward and patted the bed next to me. Some hurried whispers followed. Then the shadows examined the bed where I slept. I saw the faces then. The Goose and another. They were pained faces. Wretched.

    "Hey, Bud," whispered the Goose, nudging me. "Yer in <u>my</u> bed."

    "Oh! I must have counted wrong in the dark," I muttered, and rolled over.

    My last recollection was of Jack sobbing by my bed (the right one, that is) while he and the other shook the sheets and re-made the bed. On the floor I heard the patter of tiny feet. Mice, I think; and the rattle of falling crumbs.

    You don't understand, do you.

    No wonder Kathrine Mansfield sobbed on every page of her journal. "I can't get anything written." How can you write other things if you spend all your time on a journal?

[Drawing: (The philosopher)]

When I have a child I shall give him white shoes as soon as he learns to kick his feet. Everybody who is somebody wears white shoes. I can't afford a fraternity, but by goss I'm getting my white bucks tomorrow.

---

9 – October 52 – Thurs.　[For Joan's SLIM magazine]

> Here's a note to all youse freshmens:
> Compliments make good impreshens
> Shakespeare saith, when out to tea:
> "Lord, what foods these morsels be!"
>
> —Noggin Gnash

---

10 – October – 52 Friday

Moll Flanders surprised me. I thought it would be fairly blah, but . . . .

Moll Flanders is 328 (Everyman's Edition) pages of unparalleled, incomparable, unrivaled, unbelievable, uninhibited rot. A stronger, more disgusting word would fit here, but no thanx. Blame the silly representation of character upon the times, and take what's left. Blame the wandering, bouncing, impossible plot on Defoe's own full life, and take what's left. Blame the soaked handkerchiefs and red eyes on the "demand of the market for sentimentalism," and take what's left. Blame the style on the era; Blame the pettiness on conventional philosophy in the 18th century; Blame the constant hypocritical apology for sin on the censors, and then, take what's left in the book and cherish it—for it is called a great book. But what's left?

In appraising/praising the book wise men choose this passage:

"As soon as he was gone, and I had shut the door, I threw off my hood, and bursting out into tears, "My dear," says I, "Do you not know me?" He turned pale, and stood speechless, like one thunderstruck, and not able to conquer the surprise, said no more but this, "Let me sit down"; and sitting down by the table, and leaning his head on his hand, fixed his eyes on the ground as one stupid. I cried so vehemently, on the other hand, that it was a good while ere I could speak any more; but after I had given some vent to my passion by tears, I repeated the same words, "My dear, do you not know me?" At which he answered, Yes, and said no more for a good while."

Sure that's good. Fine. But in the next paragraph the author, resting after having outdone himself throws off the power of this scene by making the man (the Lancashire husband) suddenly fall passionately in love with Moll—his none-too-chaste wife—age 65 already yet, with cracks on her kisser and sunken eyes from prison life. Real sex appeal she's got. At 55 she manages to seduce a nobleman. Oh, she's got it! Now at 65—pugh! Victorianism I like, Modernism I like. Swift I like. But just between me and this line, Defoe is a clever fool. What Fielding would sneeringly call a GREAT man. And like that GREATEST of GREAT men of GREATNESS, Jonny Wild, I'd like to see Daniel "hanged by the neck till he was dead" for the time he wasted messing up the good parts of his books.

Just for fun I think I'll burlesque the passage I quoted. (Remember, Moll is 65, her spouse 60—but well preserved. Moll is a withered wreck.) (note good use of sentimentalism!)

"My dear," croaks I, "do you not know me?"

He turned pale, and started retching like one thunderstruck in the belly and, not able to conquer his odorous vomiting, said no more but this, "Let me sit down!" and sitting down by a table, he laid his elbow upon his plate of beans and potatoes, and hanging his chin off his hand, fixed his eyes on his nose as one stupid. I cried so vehemently, on the other hand, that it was a good while ere I could speak any more; but after I had given some vent to my amourous passion (for 65 is not as old as you think)

I stopped crying and let him go, saying "My dear, do you not know me?" At which he puked some more and answered, "Glurgle," and said no more for a good while.

(Note on side in margin) Like when Pope lets his disgust drown out his wit. Byron too (according to Edgar Johnson)

Oh Mother! Don't I write pretty prose! ?

Last night after coming home from a practice for the Monon audition the Goose and I climbed the brick wall of Locust Manor, crawled through the 2nd story window of Walt Black's room, and pushed a dresser against a door so that he couldn't get in.

An hour later he and Bob Price brought to us — very formally, without comment — this note:

[Drawing]

—**Censored**—

that's the way it goes. Sorry, hadda tear it out.

Walt din't approve.

Idea for Showdown:

The Student principle (al?)

Bavaria U.   No drinking on campus

New prex   2 scenes

pretty secretary

ugly hag (prof)

Capt. Ignuts - ex-Rotcey man

Music: from "Oklahoma"

Here's to DePauw Boys—

"MHA Sweetheart

"If you were the only—

—dance from "Prince"—

Just read W. L. Phelps' appraisal of Moll Flanders. But I don't care. W. L.P. is a great man, probably my favorite critic because of his book on Browning. Still, as long as Mark Twain can say "any collection of books is a good one as long as it doesn't include the Vicar of Wakefield." Well, I like that book, but that's my feeling on Moll. A pox on Mrs. Flanders. May it be cursed by future generations until it dies an utterly ignominious death. So there.

(It's two a.m.—October 10—but never mind, we won't make this a new entry.

Wm L. Phelps is great. Oh, he doesn't like Fielding either. (I do). Says "H.F. did more harm to the development of the novel than any other single monster" [with a pen]. To me, Fielding is tops. So it goes.

But WLP is an awfully clever satirist in his own right. Forinstance:

"Now the 18th-century fashonable girl was most gentle, most proper, most retiring. Her chief charm was delicacy; and if she had a touch of tuberculosis, she became irresistible."

Oh that's great and good.

He says also that a real novel is "a good story well told." I think I have read 4 (four) real novels, 2 by Dickens. (Maybe that's too cruel.) (No, I forgot Jane Austen's stuff.)

WLP also, satirically, says:

[passage like] "on one occasion her little foot moved, " altho' she had been carefully taught too that even this beautiful portion of the female frame should be quiet and unobtrusive. "Many readers politely surmise that Cooper was an ass."

Me, too.

Glanced thru Rasselas. The good Dr. Johnson was no novelist. Great maybe (as Fielding looked on greatness) but as a novelist. A drip.

You know, this unguided reading of mine is bad, I fear. I just decide, all by myself, that a guy is peutrid (?). But I never really know. Ah me.

Goodbye sweet book.

This is the way the world ends

"   "   "   "   "   "   "

"   "   "   "   "   "   "

Not with a bang but a whimper.

Oct. 10 —

       for Joan's paper in St. Louis Inst. of Music

       To you with wide eyes and blank address books

       you who haven't flunked one yet

       you who cringe beneath the white-fanged soph'more

       to you we dedicate this first issue

You can see that I'm really a <u>prose</u> writer. I write verse with my <u>left</u> foot.

Oct. 11—

   —<u>THE</u> <u>LOVING</u> <u>FRIENDS</u>—   —INCIDENT—

Ollie's boy

The Thompsons:

Uncle Jim [Dead]

     Aunt Lill

     John - Grampa

     Anne - Gramma

     Gran - uncle

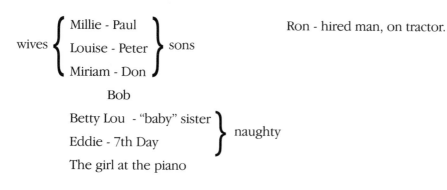

wives {
  Millie - Paul
  Louise - Peter
  Miriam - Don
} sons

Ron - hired man, on tractor.

Bob

Betty Lou - "baby" sister
Eddie - 7th Day
} naughty

The girl at the piano

Jack
Paulie
Sally
Betty
Bobby
} kids

1. Sullen, naturalistic
2. two views
3. Good + bad mixed up
4. Burlesque in blues

2 collies

Lill: "It's so good to have one's friends around, times like this." She meant it. Her sunken eyes were too (tired) to support politeness.

"Yes, It must be very nice," I said.

The Vision of St. Hilda

Story

Terrible Irony

"Sympathetic" approach

Hilda can't walk . . . . musc dyst?

Sees a vision, can, now (but doesn't bother?)

House? becomes shrine

2 statues—old priest teaches her Latin

the people on the road. Love story, handsome young man needs—help in Latin. Boat ride.

the doctor (protestant)

Pneumonia—Hilda dies

Sainted. Close with beauty of shrine [Box]

Contrast

Dialogue

Narrative

etc.,.

[Drawing]

Oct. 12 —

In the craft book Dr. Pence again and again begged the student to work hard, for his teacher's time is valuable. Someday I will write a book asking the prof to have some pity on the poor student, who can't afford to waste hours listening to a lot of conversational gaiety over stuff that's in the book. The air would be quite profitably used on bubble gum.

This crime—boring the student—is especially common in the ROTC department, but there it is forgivable. The student is suffering in class instead of on the battle-field. However, our fine English department has traces of the practice.

For instance: 45 minutes in a course on Lit covered these subjects, as my notes show:

1. Various degrees, honors, robes, etc., bestowed upon students in some English and American colleges (with a detailed account of how hot it was back in 19—)

2. The school colors of Wooster, DePauw, Harvard, Yale and some others. (I couldn't keep up, but hope to get my notes from a fellow next to me.)

3. Reasons why smoking will be permitted in this class, with a hurried history of the freedom here allowed.

4. The financial push by the Alums. This is it as I understand it. DPU wants money; a lot of it. (What if a depression hits—but of course, these are wise men, all wise men, and I have no right to comment). Well the Alums must start a campaign to get themselves to give generously. Naturally to start a thing of this import the school must have a roarin' good party as a send-off. But since no one but the Alums can afford it, they will finance the party that is supposed to put themselves in a mood to give drunkenly. Who but a college man could devise such a powerful plan. Irresistable, I call it.

5. If you see an important personage, run up to him and shake his hand. He <u>wants</u> to know you. (That's not bad, but unfortunately, in polite society, this kind of action is generally considered the mark of an odd-ball,—well, I betcha plenty of lovely chaps will take the good diety's advice and say, "Hello, doctor. I am Percival Abbington Northingly the fourth, from Muncie. Ind. I am a Tau Kappa Epsilon, and plan to make a 3.00 average. I am a vergin. I never drink. Here, take one of my cards.")

6. See a <u>REAL</u>, <u>LIVE</u> Nobel Prize WINNER! FREEE!

The only D.P.U. Nobel Prize WINNER in captivity!

7. Never forget a word one of those intellectual, outstanding, swell, real fine personages say. They sat up all last week thinking of it, and they know how to deliver it. Yeah man.

    Then of course there's another prof in the Eng. dept. Y'know, when I get big, daddy, I wanna be like Proffessor Gigglebumps. An instructor of her rank and bearing has not only the priviledge of boring her students to distraction, but also of channeling full concentration upon the uninteresting subject at hand. Hence, the student cannot share his misery with a passing bird or spider or decorded (?) senior running home. P.S. Dear teach, I'll get you, come showdown. You WAIT!

[Vertically, along margin of the above full paragraph]
—SEE NEXT PAGE—

(Oct. – 13)

Dear me, page 30, you look cross. I'll bet you really believed all that stuff I wrote yesterday. Remember, from now on "Lies, Lies, Lies" and don't be hurt so easily. I swear, you're the temperamentalest paper I've ever written on. I use a naughty word and you sulk till I blot it out. I sound mad and you pout. All right, all right! I'm sorry. And besides I lost the Monon yesterday. You'd be mad too. Ya see, the guy who won, won last year. A good writer. But his book was only half finished, and his music just started. What music he had was so bad that the young judges got Beth, my partner, to re-write it for him. Too bad, isn't it. I was rather pulling for John Jakes'. Bob Zemon's might have been an awful flop, but I thought it was funny. So did the judges. Alas, against the advice of the advisors, our girls picked John's (D). For John D is sparkling and bright. He better be brighter than last year. I'm sorry for the girls though. Somebody may find out they are all dating in John's frat house. They won't understand. They'll be nasty!. But not I!. I'm virtuousk!

Speaking of Lies, "All the world loves a lover" is a lie, by goss.

[Drawing]

[Before we go into this let me explain my method. I, when stating a discussion of this nature, love to choose the side which seems wrong but isn't. You see, I come from a long line of harrangers. Lawyers, preachers, philosophers, professors, and fish-mongers. Well, in developing my arguments I like to convince you that I'm dead wrong by using weak arguments, unnecessary sarcasm, and bad illustrations. Then, after pages of this, I come to one sensible argument. Sometimes I forget that one by the time I reach it, but I don't care who wins. It's the joy of jousting I'm out for.]

I'm a normal fellow, and lovers disgust me. In life, of course, they're too ridiculous to have any place in a work of this paper's intellectual caliber. But even in literature I can't stan' em. I, personally, am madly in love with a sweet li'l red-head. She is the finest girl in the world, and I'm marrying her in June. But if you are sensible, you'll laugh at me, just as I would at you. Behold my case a moment longer. Me, I'm so thin and delicate that a dischord between two tricycle horns could transform my body mass to a weak electrical impulse. Joan outweighs me by ten pounds, at least. Me, I can't remember my way back to Locust from the union building, I'm that dull. Joan is finishing both SLIM and W.U. in a year. Looking at it sensibly, isn't it crazy? But I like the girl.

Now look at literature. Name your lover and I'll laugh at her. (Don't name Romio and Juliet though. Joolie was only 13, as I recall, and I'm not sure she knew what was coming off.)

Of course there are Grace Livingston Hill characters like Seagrave and Emily (who reek with purity). "'Seagrave, dear,' she said, venturing to touch his smooth white hand." I'm in hysterics already.

Or there's Stienbeck, where he and she (forget the names) enjoy each other on a dead woman's cold corpse. (Course Stienbeck wants you to be a little disgusted, methinks.

And there's the Saturday Evening Post.

I'm getting tired of this. But note how seldom you <u>believe</u> a guy will really love till death his gal when he swears he will. I guess only a lover loves a lover, and even then, I laugh at everybody but me. Gad I'm a disgusting cuss!! ya can do that in a journal.

I'm ashamed of myself. All this vulgar talk in such a nice book! I'll buy a new pen and balance this trash with good. But first, "one lawst fling!"

Eve, she was a merry soul;*

*Writ by Hal Peterson for our "Back to <u>Natural</u> Sin" campaign. (No drinking, no swearing, no smoking. Just sex.)

And so was Adam, on the whole, Gad, I can't stand it. I can not look at such sinful rot. I'll turn to a new page.

Oct. 23, 1952 – Thursday

Henry Fielding was a great guy. Phelps says he slowed down the progress of the novel by advocating digressions at the beginning of each book in a work. Me, I wish novelists would do it some more. Those digressions don't in the least tempt me to skip. They build suspense, and at the same time please me with their thoughtfulness. His books become one long (886 pages for Tom Jones) essay. Never at any time does the author leave the stage. He becomes a sage with a $3 seat making clever comments as the play progresses. Reading Fielding is like going to a good play with someone who knows it well. Between the acts we have delicious commentary on the thing. It's <u>great</u>. I swear, if I can ever become a writer (and I can't because I like this sort of thing) I shall— when my fame is established—take up the style of Fielding.

George Saintsbury, or some equally tiresome critic, once said that "when novelists realized the importance of what they were doing, they stepped away from the lights and let their characters take over." In other words, men like Fielding, were just playing around, and accidentally started the literary ball rolling. By George, tain't so. Fielding I think, must have been pretty doggone serious about his work. And what he has to say is, to him, and to me, as important as anything later novelists wrote. He had, furthermore, a more servicable? tool than those writers had. While they must put all their ideas into the mouths of characters—a limitation which brought about many of the long, dull soliloquies (?) found in later (and earlier) works—Fielding could keep his characters human, and now and then step in to say a few words himself.

Other critics have said that Fielding was too intellectual, too cold, to write convincingly of love. Oh was he? I'll not copy here the passage from Tom Jones wherein

Tom finds Sophia with a bloody nose (inflicted by her pa) and they share their beautiful sorrows—but there is no more touching scene in Goldsmith, or, for that matter, in Jane Austin.

Gad, I sound like a school boy who has just discovered <u>The Little Prince</u>. Well, I don't care. Fielding is not as bad as they say.

And neither is Mickey Spillane. By gol, the man is gifted. Compared to Trollip (?) or, for my money, Defoe (now there's a rash statement) he's a genius. Mickey boy can describe. Mickey boy can tell a story. (Granted, you've heard the story before.) If Mickey Spittoon has any fault, it is that he writes the wrong kind of book, for the wrong kind of publisher. Cloth binding would make Spillane a "great American author."

1) He writes romances. His villans are all bad, or nearly. 2.) He writes the kind of book that we're not supposed to have any more, "purpose novels," or books to teach a lesson. Fielding did it—but now days we realize that problems are too big to be answered in one book—especially a book of <u>modern</u> novel length. So he's wrong there. But there <u>are</u> such books. (<u>New Wives for Old</u>, is one, I think). I've never heard anybody who has read a Spillane book criticize it as I have here. That is to say, only those who have heard <u>about</u> him laugh at 'im. Correction: "Great" critics call him pulp. (The same "great" critics called <u>The Naked & the Dead</u> the "greatest story to come out of the war." Bull, I say. Anyway, Mickey is not so bad. As someone has said, he's "The highest of the lowest." To me, that's higher than the lowest of the highest.

[Drawings]

Maybe sex is wicked stuff
But weep for him who's had enough

You may think that sex is silly;
Try it, sis, next time yer chilly.

Frost sayeth (saith?)

The Last Word of a Bluebird.
As told to a Child

As I went out a Crow

In a low voice said, "Oh,

I was looking for you

How do you do?

I just came to tell you

To tell Lesley (will you?)

That her little Bluebird

Wanted me to bring word

That the north wind last night

That made the stars bright

And made ice on the trough

Almost made him cough

His tail feathers off.

He just had to fly!

But he sent her Good-bye,

and said to be good,

And wear her red hood,

And look for skunk tracks

In the snow with an axe—

And do everything!

And perhaps in the spring

He would come back and sing

Quite a man, R. Frost. This is, shall we say, not quite like some of his things. Versitle boy!

Carlyle in Sartor Resortus says somplace (I've forgotten where) that war is stupid. He proposes a new plan whereby the two leading generals will "in person, take each a Tobacco pipe filled with brimstone; light the same, and smoke in one another's faces till the weaker gives in;"

But from this man has learned no lesson. Carlyle wrote long ago, and wars are still our #1 international sport.

Fielding says men should fight their wars with naught but the implements God gave them, namely fists, fingernails, teeth and tongues. Then, after the battle, the dead could rise up and walk (albeit in shame) home to their women.

Nobody lissent to him either.

Funny peculiar, isn't it, that we universally agree with both these gentlemen but can't get out of our trench.

On a small scale, sending bibles and missionaries would be silly as a preclusion of war. Yet even the hardest jingoist will agree that if we spent the money we spend on war on plows, teachers, tractors, bibles, fertilizers, and How to Make Friends and Influence People books, we could end this idiotic strife. Man isn't a very practical creature.

If you tell me that I can do my math in 1/5 the time with your new slide rule, and prove it to me, I'll thank you from the bottom of my heart, buy your gadget, and, in all probability, put the thing in a drawer—or sell it for 25¢ more than it cost me. So it goes. T. S. Eliot would fit in here nicely, but I'm going to bed. G'nite sweet pages (as Oscar Wilde would say).

Oct. 27 – 52

One grows tired of little thoughts, after a while, just as one grows tired of laughing. And yet there are no big thoughts. There are only memories, pictures of people who <u>could</u> have big thoughts. Dad—Mr. Reisor—Little kids not old enought to know that it's all a big joke. There are serious places—like thin spots on an old old shirt. But pull on a new checked jacket. Hide the frayed edges. Laugh some more. There are no big thoughts for small minds—and yet, you can take the humor out of a little thought—look at it honestly—make it a little bigger. Like—

> Bird on a dead tree
> How can you sing
> Can a bird see
> —Long before me—
> Spring?

There are pictures, too. Thanks, God, for pictures. You can look at things and know that they have in them a big thought—only you can't quite catch it. Still, you can look at it and know that there is a big thought there. There are stories—like Grapes of Wrath that imply big answers—but you can't quite catch 'em. Books like Of Mice and Men; like Clarissa; like Darkness at Noon. Pictures—and things outdoors. Like—

> Tammerack
> There's power in the word, don't you think?
> Power in the word, as in the tree.
> Power from the thunder-bolt that fell.
> And split it end for end last spring.
> Belly northward now it stands.
> Grim. Reared for war.
> Sixty long-haired arms stretched out.
> Patient, sullen.
> Waiting for the storm.

Oct. 31 or so. I can't keep track of insignificant details.

A mood is with me. I have lots of interesting moods; but this one has been with me so much of late that I can't clearly remember the faces of the other ones. This mood has stepped out of me, become more real than myself. He sits over there in my chair reading Clarissa and chain smoking my cigarettes. The book is propped in his lap—his feet are on my bookcase—and with a free hand he teases the blotches on his face.

Now and then he glances up at me with a smile that may be meant to mock. "Whatter you laughing at?" I say, and he grins wide and says "something I read," and he looks at me cornerwise so I know he's lying.

It's queer—sitting here looking at a mood. Sitting in one corner of a room look- ing at a part of yourself that has stepped out and taken life for itself. He blows smoke at the page. It bounces, spreads out, out until it is air. He exhales again, and sucks the white cloud back through his nose. And I would like a cigarette but I have none. I am over here without cigarettes; maybe I haven't even life. It seems as though I've given up to the mood. Given it my name, my chair, my book, my life, my cigarettes.

The mood is laziness; or no, cleverness. I don't know what it is. But it's mighty convincing. It tells me I'm a fool, and more than that, college is a national lie. Our fine land abounds with wretches who have been to college. But they know nothing. I have here a pile of good books. Some of them I've read. I know that if I could read those books I would be wise. All wise. I have an idea about satire. I know that if I were given one year I could write a book on satire in the English novel, 1704–1900; a book that has never been written; a book that must be written someday, for all criti- cal studies of the English novel must be based on a good knowledge of my subject. The whole evolution of the novel rests on the genius of satire. Satire was the sperm that bought Mme. Epic her incomparable infant, the novel. I have it all organized. But I must read and read and read. I can't, you know. I have to go to Chemistry for five hours each week to do a few score experiments, every one of which I can al- ready explain all phases of procedure & result. I must stand for five horribly dull hours <u>each</u> week studying something I already have studied, so that I can get university credit—dear, precious stuff. I must spend fifty minutes[1] per week standing in my shorts learning how to exercize and "keep fit." This when I could be reading good stories from Balzac (which I haven't in two years found time to read) or putting into practice what I've picked up out of the latter chapters of a craft book by Uzzle.

That mood is leering again. What would you have me do, mood? I can't flunk out. It would be silly. And yet, to pass everything is to bow to the "hurry-thru-this-just-so-you-can-pass-the-test" boys. I don't want your slimy degrees. I want stuff I can use when I want to write. You won't make a Koch out of me, so why this nonsense. While you stand over me commenting on my sloppy lab procedure, Guilluam Le Bel is inventing pencilcillin—a new, cheaper, wonder drug. All departments standardize their courses for the good & the poor, the major & the minor. But these things are all <u>little</u> difficulties. The important thing is, I haven't any cigarettes.

I'm sorry that DePauwites in general are so clever. I'd write this as a satire, but I'm tired and too much satire, even my own, nausiates me. The play tonight was not very good. I admit it. The actors all missed the boat, probably. But the student critics missed it by a far greater margin. I went with two very fine fellows—intellectuals, for whom I have nothing but respect. Really. But at the end of the second act they left, and, ever since, they have been laughing at the "putrid production." I have been to plenty of plays—amatuer and professional. I am sorry that a good play must get its laughs from sex and drunkenness, but <u>still</u> I don't like the hi brow criticisms I have to sit through when it's all over. It is an acknowledged fact, no doubt, that one cannot criticise a play unless he knows a great deal about dramatics. So he who finds nothing but fault must indeed be a very clever critic. I'm guilty too, I know. Seldom can I sit through a French horn recital. I know French horn. I'm a damn good cornist. I won't apologize. So I find fault, and in so doing become an example of what I have said here. You gotta know your subject to criticise it. But it seems to me an awful lot of the dramatic critics floating around this campus—floating—it's no cliche here.

---

[1] 25 min. perday, counting dressing time)

They're really up there—a lot of 'em don't know beans. And to sound like they do, they must criticise. Now I say that the third scene of tonight's play was darn well written. Those lines didn't need an actor behind them. True, they didn't have one. But when I speak of the play I speak of the lines and "accidentaly" omit mention of the actors. The lines left me teary, and by george I'm no sentimental bastard. It was a good play. The prologue was too long—that is, the first two acts—but the play was good. Hell with the acting. The kids aren't actors. Face it. I feel sorry for the guys who left before the play—that is—the third act—started. And I'm still sorrier for the schmucks who noticed the ham that flavored those good lines. I'm sorry for the recognized "great writer" who said the lines were a "prostitution of art—merely stuck on as tear jerkers. For the love of Mike, man, did Clarissa die to make the story sell better? Did Hamlet? Did Mr. Bremble go mad so that I would read the book? Did Medea kill her kids so the tickets could be sold for more? How 'bout Anna Karaninna? or Raskolnikov? Don't feed me that spinach about lines stuck in to sell the play. I won't eat. I'll retch. (This is getting violent; dear, dear.) I like to hear a good critic speak. I hate to listen to intellectual hypocrites. And usually I manage to forget even what our good critic said. I never read reviews. They bore me. Make me tired as the devil in a WCTU meeting. (Although that good gentleman must be commended for the good work he does there in spite of the ladies' good intentions.) I admit I almost left early. But I didn't. Hooray for me. So much for you, noble critics.

[Drawing]

Afterthought (Long after): What would this have been like if I'd waited for it to cool? Obviously in anything but a journal, I'd have to.

[Drawing: Trying to Recinize "Jr." (Dad's Day Review—Nov. 1, 1952)]

Nov. 5th

"As for the motto . . . I desire that it may not be engraved in the Greek and Latin lingoes . . . but in plain English, that when the angel comes to pipe <u>all hands</u> at the great day, he may know that I am a British man, and speak to me in my mother tongue."—Smollett

Nov. 6 –

Here I go, making another dull and trite observation. But no matter how often a phenominon has been observed in the past, it is always worthwhile to observe it again. Otherwise, why do we have elementary chemistry, or sermons 52 Sundays a year?

If a society were completely happy it would be completely stupid. That is, completely witless, dull mentally,—without understanding. For when we are happy we just can't think. Period. We float on our joy and any serious thought is beneath us. The men who make great advances, the men who make sage observations, are the suffering Carlyles: the rhumatic Mathiew Brambles: the oppressed Dostiefskis, the hypocondriactic Johnsons. A happy, (with a child-like happiness) serene fellows have nothing to say. Their only mode of expression is a sigh—and who can sit down for an hour and converse with a sigh? Grace Livingston Hill was exaultant in her religious joy. Her books show it. Her chapters are happy sighs that show a feeling, but, in analysis, contain little more than happily exhaled air. Katherine Mansfield, on the other hand, has a sound, intellectual religion, not based on white clouds and yellow flowers, but on a racking cough, a headache, blood in the throat.

I have been trying all day to study, but I'll be darned if I can (It's warm outside; my girl loves me; Dad sent $5; I got an A on a theme; Pence called me "discerning"; I got a paper published.) I can see that Humphrey Clinker has certainly got it rough, but

I don't much care. I can see that Swift is right, we're all bastards, but I kinda enjoy it. I can see that there can be no afterlife, as Kostler maintains, but I still look foreward to it.

Now you may think that this is just observation, and stupider than the society I talked of in the beginning. Well, if I left it at observation, it would be awful, rotten, retched writing. So what is the practical application?

Well, in the first place, we can build our world on it. That's a very impressive application. And, I might say, a popular one thru the ages, for every observation of a philosophical nature. We can have the most supremely intellecual society in the history of the world. How?

1. Inflict pain upon everybody. Raise taxes, outlaw dirty jokes; Raise the comp. education limit to 35. etc. Make em unhappy; for from dissatisfaction & sorrow comes thought.

2. Revise the educational system. (The object of the present one is, it seems to me, give 'em a good time.) Make the prime objective a souring of soul which will result in works of genius to outshine Dante's <u>Inferno</u>, Carlyle's bitterest books, Swift himself.

3. Save time. Cut out the sabbath by cutting out religion which gives pleasure. Then, since there are 365.257 days in an astronomical year we will give philosophers and mathematicians great sorrows in trying to divide that number by six. People will die of overwork, which will inflict more sorrow (they get no vacations on Sunday.)

Now I'll tell you a secret. I have proved my original point. You can't think sensibly when yer happy. Unfortunately, I'm happy. It's a horrible feeling, but, I hope, it has almost left me.

Nov. 8th

Last year Crandall said that the primary difference between man and monkey is the homo sapiens' thumb. He said that a child was raised with an exactly the same age monkey. They developed at the same rate until the thumb got in the way. The monkey couldn't create with blocks or crayons (etc) because he couldn't grasp things. He hadda scoop 'em. Well, suppose that an extremely intelligent ape were given (by medical means) a human thumb. Suppose he developed as a man.—Great fictional possibilities, eh? The doctor treats the ape as a son—etc. etc—But at last the ape falls in love with a human female. Great eh? Ha ha!

Nov 13

    Here's a note to you who speak or write:
    Verbocity's a thing you've got to fight.
    Shakespeare saith of lecturers & such
    Me thinks my laddie doth express too much.

20 November 52

I hate William Makepeace Thackeray with a beautiful, blooddripping hate. And I think R. W. Pence is an inferior Lit teacher. (Which has no connection except that both men are damn egoists.) What did Thackeray ever do that had any good use whatsoever? He developed an idea about how books should be written, and by whom (meaning fine men of the upper class—like himself); and proceeded to write Vanity Fair, Henry Esmond, and a batch of other stupid[1] novels. Then, still hunting for a field in which to show his talents he took up slandering greater authors than himself. A critic is an angry author who lives in a house made of reject slips, or else a vain bastard who'll do anything to make an appearance before his dear public. [Marginal Note: G.K. Chesterson is one of these—I've only read his bull on Browning but that is utter rot.] Once in a while—one or two per century—a real scholar honestly turns adventurer and names himself a critic. (Saintsbury)

I don't know which of these Thackeray was, but he certainly had the fingernails for the job! I hate iz guts, I do. And because W. M. T. dislikes them, I love Sterne and Swift, and guys like that. Thackeray is one of the most vulgar, nauseus, cruel, inhuman, slanderous, simple-minded, malevolent, malignant, morbid, caustic, ill-informed, opinionated, dogmatic, debased, impolite, and egotistic Yahoos that ever lived. He says of Swift:

"Would you have liked to be a friend of the great Dean? . . . If you had been his inferior in parts . . . his equal in mere social station, he would have bullied, scorned, and insulted you; if, undeterred by his great reputation, you had met him like a man, he would have quailed before you, and not had the pluck to reply, and gone home, and years later written a foul epigram about you—watched for you in a sewer, and come out to assail you with a coward's blow and a dirty bludgeon." That's about all the ink I can spend on that kind of (I need a word here. Something like dung but more polite—more cutting.) . . .

Since I have not the stomach to go on and copy more (though all of Thackeray's essay on Swift is like this—demoniacal) let me analyze the sneakiness, the petty hatefulness in W. M. T.

The part about—he would have bullied, scorned, insulted you. This is ridiculous. Swift was noted for his genius at making friends of both sexes. So W. M. T.

---

1. No slight meant here. They may be very nice novels in most respects. But to me they are tripe. Charming, moving, interesting—maybe, but mostly just stoopud.

disregards this fact and attacks one or two isolated incidents found in Swift's biographies—The Earl of Orerry, Scott, Sheridan, Johnson—everybody that wrote was so perplexed by a few of Swift's most cutting satires that the biographies changed their whole mood. Swift's light repartee was twisted and given ominous significance—even called madness in the 19th century. And all these things Thackeray pounced upon, blew up, until he could say "—as if the wretch who lay under that stone waiting God's judgment had a right to be angry." To Thackeray I say in the words of Grenidine etching "I spit in the milk of your grandmother."

When Defoe aimed his Thackeray-like blasts at "the learned Dr. S——" the good Dean didn't even bother to answer—that's how misanthropic he was on a <u>personal</u> scale. Then when he wanted to defend a later work he remembered the dig and casually mentioned the "fellow who was pilloried." This, I take it, is the "foul epigram" W. M. T. speaks of. Or no, Since Defoe was a lower-class man it must have been someone else. But the principle is the same. Ah well.

Education and learning are enemies of one another. The above tirade is an example of this. [By education I mean the passing of tests etc. which win a man the epithit "scholar." Learning I consider the acquirement of knowledge.] Now in a lit course none of this information[1]. is of any particular value.

One must know dates, facts, statistics. Obviously, the more time spent in memorizing facts, the less time left for mere research. [That's why spelling is a crime. Students spend the best years of their lives learning to spell instead of thinking and exploring so that they have something to say with the words that they can spell.] Our system of education not only absorbs so much of the student's time that he can't stop to discover anything, but it actually encourages him to forget about thinking and spend his time memorizing. This falacy has sundry ramifications: politics are ill founded; polititions are accepted on faith; old ideas—like the physical electrical

---

1. (The above tirade)

current that goes the wrong way—last 4 centuries after they've been disproved. Religion, which is enclined to be dogmatic, makes no advances, unless there are advances backward.

But I digress even more than one should in a half-assed book like this. I started this present discussion to lead up to my ideas of <u>Gulliver</u>, which I can't work into any <u>real</u> school work cause I'm so darn radical. Rather I must know that <u>Gulliver</u> in 1718–1720*, published in 1726, corrected in 1727, and again in the 3rd edition (Fulkner's first) in 1728; first standered in September 1726 by (I forgot the name) a pamphlet that Johnson got a hold of and made into his commentary on Swift. Down with such rot!

Because I have a natural love for argumentation, and because it is the popular 20th century mode to defend the slandered author and scratch the exaulted, I immediately started hunting up defences for Swift. There are surprisingly numerous defenses possible. I say that Swift was a <u>nice</u> guy. The fourth book of Gulliver which slams mankind, I explain by saying Swift was a preacher, a cleric, a divine. It is not the business of such a man to commend society. It is his duty to point out its failings. (This is a matter of self-preservation, for if clerics admit man is fine they have no reason to offer Redemption, so there.) So now an analysis of <u>Gulliver</u> as a lay reader (me) sees it, without all the trenchent wit, the ironic stink, the dirrogatory nonsense:

Say I: In <u>Gulliver's Travels</u> there are four books, and three distinct satirical aims. Books I and II, Gulliver's journeys to Lilliput and Brobdingnag, satirize government from two points of view. Book III, the trip to Laputa, etc., satirizes education and knowledge. Book IV, the trip to Honyhnhnmland points out human failings.

In Lilliput Lemuel Gulliver was nearly thirteen times as tall as the king (a giant himself, <u>almost a fingernail width taller than his tallest subjects!</u>) From this great height it was easy to see the whole scheme of Lilliputian life and politics. The philosophical, political, and social question of how to break an egg, while it seems vital to

---

* After the Tory fall of 1714 when Swift was pushed back to Ireland.

the Lilliputan appears to Gulliver in its true ridiculous light. The selfishness of princes; the prudishness carried to extremes, seen in the result of Gulliver's philan-thropic battle with the palace fire; the duplicity of courts; the misconcieved egoism of the tiny lords all show up plainly to the omniscient mountain-top eye.

Swift's irony flows continually, as Saintsbury has said, but let us note a few of his brilliant thrusts. When first the "tall" monarch appeared, Gulliver notes that: "He held his sword drawn in his hand, <u>to defend himself</u>, <u>if I should happen to break loose</u>;" (italics mine.) "it was almost three inches long . . . " What a beautiful, tragic, hilarious picture of man, proud, vainglorious!

A little later Gulliver witnesses a competition for a vacated office in the Lilliputan Royal Court. Gulliver says:

> "—five or six . . . candidates petition the Emperor to entertain his Majesty and the court with a dance on the rope, and whoever jumps the highest without falling, succeeds in the office. Very often the chief ministers themselves are commanded to show their skill, and to convince the Emperor that they have not lost their faculty. Flimnap, the Treasurer, is allowed to cut a caper on a straight rope, at least an inch higher than any other lord in the whole empire. I have seen him do the summerset several times together upon a trencher fixed on the rope, which is no thicker than a common pack thread in England."

Note also the delicious satire in the discussion of the three fine silken threads a blue, a red, and a green, conferred as a favor by the Emperor.

Then there's the episode of the monarch's insatiable greed for more ships after Gulliver has captured 60 longboats.

But I must hurry. I have my French to do. (Education vs. learning again.)

In the second book Gulliver gets the opposite point of view. The Brobdingnagians, 60' tall are seen in exact detail. Perfumes are so strong that Gulliver faints beneath them. Here, through irony, he points out the littleness, the pettiness of his own type government & reasoning compared to theirs. These two books then, attack govern-ment, primarily.

The Lapatuans, with their love of science & music; their intolerance of the old in their search for the new, glorious truth; their absorbtion in thought (so great that they need rattles for conversation) which produces nothing—all these blast English study and ridiculous patronage of new, new, <u>new</u> ideas, whether tried or not.

Now for Book IV: Critics say that—well, Orerry said, "Swift's misanthropy is intolerable. The representaion which he has given us of human nature, must terrify, and even debase the mind of the reader who views it." Critics call swift a monster because he pointed out the sins of man. In one place Swift (or rather Gulliver) attacks man by saying that in Houyhnhnmland "I did not feel the treachery or inconstancy of a friend, nor the injuries of a secret or open enemy. I had no occasion of bribing, flattering, or pimping to procure the favor of any great man or of his minion. I wanted no fence against fraud or oppression; here was neither physician to destroy my body, nor lawyer to ruin my fortune; no informer to watch my words and actions, or forge accusations against me for hire; here were no gibers, censurers, backbiters, pickpockets, highwaymen, housebreakers, attorneys, bawds, buffoons, gamesters, politicians, wits, splenetics, tedious talkers, controvertists, ravishers, murderers, robbers, virtuosos; no leaders or followers of party and faction; no encourager to vice, by seducement or example; no dungeon, axes, gibbets, whipping-posts, or pillories; no cheating shopkeepers or mechanics; no pride, vanity, or affectation; no fops, bullies, drunkards, strolling whores, or poxes; no ranting, lewd, expensive wives; no stupid, proud pedants" (are you listening WMT?) "no importunate, overbearing, quarrelsome, noisy, roaring, empty, conceited, swearing companions; no scoundrels, raised from the dust for the sake of their vices, or nobility thrown into it on account of their virtues; no lords, fiddlers, judges, or dancing-masters."

The critics may scream that Swift has painted a foul picture, call it "symptomatic of mental desease," but they will not forget it; and once in a while they will find themselves doing something touched in that list. Will they not be nauseated at a realization that <u>they</u> are damnable <u>Yahoos</u>? Is not this restraint due to self-contempt higher than restraint as a result of "Hell fire preaching?" Swift does not bawl, like so many divines about punishments in the next life; he points his finger, frowns and administers punishment through concience in <u>this</u> one. Isn't he, then, a <u>great</u> preacher? Call him insane. But there is still an <u>unparalleled</u> scolding in Book IV; and certainly no preacher ever reached a wider audience than Swift. John Wesley complained that it was, in his day (he was a contemperary of Swift) "quite out of fasheon to suggest that humanity [was] all wise, all innocent" etc.

.˙. (And now I go to my French) Hail Swift! and Hail with Thackeray, and all the vampires that called out that noble vulture.

November 29: —Fragment—

. . . It is an evil night.

Fog lies writing in the streets

. . . the green white soul of some huge monster,

Newly dead of poison.

Nov. 31: How stoopid

Dec. 9, 1952 yet still.

I went to a party.

It was an ordinary party, you might say except for a few little things. It was a birthday party but it was over a month late because we who threw the party happened to be broke when Ben's birthday came. So nobody even said "Happy birthday' on that <u>real</u> day. Also it was held in a laundry. I don't know that this is unusual, but it was new to me. Madame Beauret, with whom Ben stays, is a connisseur de handker-chief. She does fine cleaning for fine (or at least rich) people. She is not very well-to-do herself, so she couldn't afford to fix up both her home and her business. (Her husband died in France in 1916, I think. There's a plaque of medals with French words on em hanging in Madam's living room—upstairs from the laundry.) As I was saying, since she's not rich herself, and must cater (or rather prefers to cater) to the upper set, she has put all her money to the laundry. As a result that part of the building is beautiful, with a red red rug, a dazzling glass counter and five or six huge, leather armchairs. Hence, we had the party there instead of upstairs. Another slightly unusual thing—It was a surprise party, and Ben, who could not be tricked into going down to the laundry to be surprised was finally heaved down the chute bodily. You should have seen his jolly face when he phuglmphed into the clothes pile to the tune of Happy birthday to you.

Ben and all of the party (—except myself who am devorced from such things since I gave away my French horn) were musicians of the first order. Ben had hardly disentangled himself before the party began to beat on Mario Lanza. By shorting a steam iron Guy got his tape machine to work and we sat on bundles and on the floor, and a few of us on the cake my love tried to make, to hear the horriblest of singers sing at some lovely song.

I kind of liked it.

There was the Beethoven 9th as Toscanni did it, too. This also I liked. There were no conductors in the crowd, so we agreed that the piece would do. Does this sound dull and insignificant? Does this bore you, make you sweat, make you fidget and curl your lip?

I wondered if it would. Mee to.

Been reading Tristram Shandy. Can't make sense of anything anymore. I've dis-covered one thing tho'. Life is no use. Man hath no dignity. If he likes a book he's dull, unoriginal, sentimental, one of the crowd. This is obviously true; but due (or thanks, if you love your grammar) to mass education everybody knows this truth; so everybody, in order to avoid dullness, dissents. So even dissention is dull.

This is such a small thought, it isn't worth condensing.

I have digressed a little, I'm afraid. I meant for this book to be a Locust Manor chronicle, but I kept slipping away into conversation and never getting to the point. I've completely missed the one and only date nite we got here. A failure: the goose and Mr. Getty plugged the chimney, and we're still finding hunks of popcorn where the lovers left them in their flyte. And there was the mock murder, and the mirror-smash, and the war we had with the hi-school boys and the time Clapp came over and lost the tires off his car, and—alas! all this is old news now. And I've forgotten the details I meant to use (honestly or otherwise).

I meant to clip in the stuff I got published at Washington U, too—but there's still lots of time for that, I guess. I can't wait to see what I wrote for this issue's editorial.

Well, this didn't undigress me, but I feel repremanded. Maybe I'll be better from now on.

I have just read this thing up to hear. Lawse I'm a bitter one! Not really though. Life isn't half bad.

And next year in Wash. U. I'll have no friends, 'cept a wife, and I can study instead of help others thru. (More bitterness. Hafta watch that.)

ACKNOWLEDGEMENTS

Lies! Lies! Lies! will be the three millionth volume to be added to the collections of the University of Rochester Libraries.

Based upon an original, unpublished manuscript from the John Gardner Archive in the Libraries' Department of Rare Books and Special Collections, the book is the product of a partnership between the Libraries and BOA Editions of Rochester, the nation's foremost publisher of books of poetry. Steve Huff and his BOA staff handled the production end; Peter Dzwonkoski, Head of the Department of Rare Books and Special Collections, oversaw the balance of the project. We are grateful to Geri McCormick, who designed the book. We would also like to acknowledge the generosity of the Libraries' friends who made it possible for the University to acquire the Gardner Archive.

Lies! Lies! Lies!

has been issued in a first edition of two thousand copies, of which two hundred numbered copies have been specially bound in French marble paper over boards and signed by Thomas Gavin, the author of the Introduction. The hardcover trade edition consists of eight hundred copies, and the remaining thousand copies have been bound in paper wrappers. The typeface is ITC Garamond.

This copy is number _____